Also by Jack Cashill

Unmasking Obama:
The Fight to Tell the True Story
of a Failed Presidency

The Hunt

BARACK OBAMA'S
PROMISED LAND
Deplorables Need Not Apply

JACK CASHILL

Post Hill
PRESS

A POST HILL PRESS BOOK
ISBN: 978-1-64293-905-7
ISBN (eBook): 978-1-64293-906-4

Barack Obama's Promised Land:
Deplorables Need Not Apply
© 2021 by Jack Cashill
All Rights Reserved

Cover art by Joel Gilbert

Post Hill Press
New York • Nashville
posthillpress.com

Published in the United States of America
1 2 3 4 5 6 7 8 9 10

To my always supportive wife, Joan Dean, the rare university professor who would have tolerated me.

Facts do not cease to exist because they are ignored.
Aldous Huxley

Contents

Preface

In no small part, Barack Obama's newest memoir, *A Promised Land*, is a tale of what Obama aptly calls "sausage making." He takes us back stage to witness the creation of TARP and the 2009 Recovery Act and the Affordable Care Act and Dodd-Frank, all of which, in his book, were successes, if not downright triumphs. He offers the same detail with his foreign policy decisions. In all of these deliberations, he pictures himself as calm, confident, reflective, prudent—the very model of a modern major president. As cool and in control as he imagines himself to be, however, Obama hides the fear that has haunted him throughout his career and that undermined his presidency.

Many of the book's reviewers, literary people for the most part, accept these details uncritically. They simply don't know enough about recent history to sort fact from fiction. What the reviewers miss—and what this book will provide—are the details that Obama omits, the major stories he has chosen to bury, and his reasons for doing both.

In editing out so much that is true, Obama spares himself any serious introspection. By refusing to understand himself, he cannot begin to understand his critics. Rush Limbaugh may have said, "I hope he fails," but in the one arena most critical to the nation's future, Limbaugh wanted Obama to succeed. So did every other conservative and centrist that I know. It was Obama's "friends" who wanted him to fail. Unfortunately for America, they had their way.

Acting Like Boys Instead of Men

On Father's Day 2008, Obama made easily his best speech on race, arguably his best speech ever.[1] The setting was the Apostolic Church of God in Chicago.

"Here at Apostolic," said Obama, after quoting from the Sermon on the Mount, "you are blessed to worship in a house that has been founded on the rock of Jesus Christ, our Lord and Savior." This is the same Lord and Savior who, alas, makes no appearance of consequence in the pages of *A Promised Land*.

"Of all the rocks upon which we build our lives, we are reminded today that family is the most important," Obama continued. "And we are called to recognize and honor how critical every father is to that foundation." Obama spoke here from the heart. More than any previous presidential memoir, *A Promised Land* is a tribute to the joys and responsibilities of fatherhood. Would that all children in America could grow up with the love and support Malia and Sasha have enjoyed. Far too many have not. Obama knew this.

"But if we are honest with ourselves," he continued, "we'll admit that what too many fathers also are is missing—missing from too many lives and too many homes. They have abandoned their responsibilities, acting like boys instead of men. And the foundations of our families are weaker because of it." Obama proceeded to explain the consequences of fatherlessness in words that his 2004 Senate opponent, Alan Keyes, might have said—words that bête noire Sarah Palin would have cheered, words that the hated Tea Party would have welcomed.

"You and I know how true this is in the African-American community," said Obama. "We know that more than half of all black children live in single-parent households, a number that has doubled—doubled—since we were children. We know the statistics—that children who grow up without a father are five times more likely to live in poverty and commit crime; nine times more likely to drop out of schools and 20 times more likely to end up in prison."[2]

Here, Obama correctly identified family breakdown—not racism, not police brutality, not even the legacy of slavery and Jim Crow—as the reason America's inner cities have become the most dangerous and dysfunctional in the developed world. This breakdown, he strongly implied, was a byproduct of the modern welfare state. Just as pointedly, Obama acknowledged that the problem was getting worse, exponentially worse. *He knew.*

On this particular Father's Day, thirteen-year-old Trayvon Martin and twelve-year-old Michael Brown had no idea they would prove out the truth of Obama's statistics. This memoir ends triumphantly with the killing of Osama bin Laden in May 2011—ten months before Trayvon would be killed in Sanford, Florida, and three years before Michael Brown would be killed in Ferguson, Missouri. Obama does not tell their stories. That's too bad because he understood what caused them to die so senselessly and so young.

On Father's Day 2008, Trayvon was likely having dinner with his father, Tracy Martin, and Tracy's second wife, Alicia Stanley. Tracy had split from Trayvon's mother, Sybrina Fulton, ten years earlier, and each had a child with another partner before they had Trayvon in 1995. Thanks to the support of "Mama 'Licia," however, Trayvon had survived his parents' divorce in better shape than many young people do. "Trayvon was in our home, 85 to 90 percent of the time," Stanley told CNN's Anderson Cooper after her stepson's death. "I'm the one that went to football games. I'm the one who was there when he was sick. I want people to know he wanted to live with me and his father."[3]

A year or so after Obama's Father's Day speech, Tracy Martin abandoned his responsibility once again and acted more like a boy than a man. He deserted Alicia and shattered the one home Trayvon could always go home to. Two years after he lost his rock, Trayvon had descended fully into a life of drugs, guns, truancy, burglary, and street fighting. The cheerful boy in the Pop Warner uniform who dreamed of becoming a pilot existed only in the nation's recklessly dishonest newsrooms. Trayvon knew he had gone wrong, and he probably knew why. His last words after being shot by the innocent man he had savagely attacked: "Tell Mama 'Licia I'm sorry."

Obama had the opportunity to set the record straight, but he chose not to. Long before Trayvon's death in 2012, Obama got the word that stories like Trayvon's were not something America needed to explore. In an election year like 2012, in a battleground state like Florida, the message of black victimization, repeated endlessly, worked much better in a stagnant economy than did hope and change.

Speaking from experience, black commentator Jesse Lee Peterson has explained why the message is so readily received. "This pattern is so obvious I am still shocked almost no one talks about it," writes Peterson in his book *The Antidote*. "It is this simple: children, black or white, when deprived of fathers, grow up angry at their parents. White children displace their anger in many different directions: suicide, bullying, and school shootings, to name a few. Black children, for the most part, channel theirs in a single destructive direction—toward and against white people."[4]

As to Michael Brown, he never really had a home. Born a year after Trayvon in 1996, his parents split up when he was three. This surely surprised no one. They were never married. His mother took him to a new neighborhood and introduced him to a succession of new "uncles." The split between Michael's parents was bitter. As he got older, Michael would call his father and ask to be "rescued."

Wrote *Esquire*'s John Richardson deep in an article blaming racism for Brown's death, "Without doubt, the turmoil in the family took its toll."[5] How could it not? At sixteen, his mother dropped Michael off at the home of his father and his new wife, a woman Michael had not even met, and left him there. Sulking, he retreated to his room and refused to go to school for three months. Uncomfortable in either household, Michael spent the last year of his troubled, angry life living with his grandmother. At least there he did not have to deal with his parents' new partners. He did, however, have to deal with shopkeepers who expected to be paid and police officers who expected to be heeded. In the last hour of his life, Brown manhandled a shopkeeper and tried to kill a cop. He must have sensed it would all end badly.

The Obama of Father's Day 2008 did not know these two young men. Although he dissembled about his own origins—"my father left us when I was 2 years old"—he told the truth about the things that mattered. "How many times in the last year has this city lost a child at the hands of another child?" he asked. "How many times have our hearts stopped in the middle of the night with the sound of a gunshot or a siren?" As Obama knew, the police sounded the sirens. Young black men, the great majority of them fatherless, produced the gunshots that prompted the sirens. "How many in this generation are we willing to lose to poverty or violence or addiction?" Obama pleaded. "How many?"

In his new memoir, *A Promised Land*, Obama shares not a word of this speech, not a hint of its message. Three weeks after giving this speech, he was told in no uncertain terms that he had overreached, that he had aspired above his pay grade. *If we are honest with ourselves*, said Obama, but he wasn't. Moral cowardice doomed his presidency and undermines his memoir. Obama continues to tell his supporters not what they need to hear, but what his progressive overlords want them to hear.

For his role in this Faustian bargain, Obama found a "promised land," of sorts, manifest most showily in his twelve-million-dollar ocean-front estate on Martha's Vineyard. As to the "Joshua generation," the post–Jim Crow generation of African Americans Obama was commissioned to lead to their promised land, these he led deeper, much deeper, into the wilderness, and he continues to mislead them still.

I Can No More Disown Him

Three months before his Father's Day speech in Chicago, Barack Obama made another speech on race. Curiously, the speech Obama wants his readers to remember is the thoroughly dishonest one he made in Philadelphia in March of 2008.[6]

At the time, Obama had a very public problem to solve, namely his relationship with firebrand Rev. Jeremiah Wright. In that this speech ends up triumphantly, at least for his campaign, Obama spends multiple pages on its genesis.[7] "I need to make a speech," he tells strategist David Plouffe. "On race. The only way to deal with this is to go big and put Reverend Wright in some kind of context. And I need to do it in the next few days."

As he does often in the book, Obama seems to accept responsibility for some fundamental flaw in his character but attaches so many qualifiers that his confession ends up sounding like a boast. "I knew the blame lay squarely on my shoulders," he writes. "I may not have been in church for any of the sermons in question or heard Reverend Wright use such explosive language. But I knew all too well the occasional spasms of anger within the Black community—my community—that Reverend Wright was channeling." To convince African Americans that their community was, in fact, "my community," Obama would need all the sophistry his white advisers and speechwriters could muster.

In March 2008, Hillary was still very much in the race. Tacking to her left, Obama loaded the Philadelphia speech with an unhealthy dose of progressive toxins. Coming from a black man "married to a black American who carries within her the blood of slaves and slave owners— an inheritance we pass on to our two precious daughters," his words had a punch Hillary couldn't counter. When Obama reminded his audience that "so many of the disparities that exist between the African-American community and the larger American community today can be traced directly to inequalities passed on from an earlier generation that suffered under the brutal legacy of slavery and Jim Crow," he identified with that community in a way Hillary never could. The speech on absent fathers would have to wait until she had been neutralized.

Still, as Obama and his advisers understood, the standard clichés would not be enough. To salvage Wright, they would have to sacrifice "Toot." Other than wife Michelle, there is no adult Obama writes about more frequently or more lovingly in this memoir than his grandmother, Madelyn Dunham. At the time of the speech, the eighty-five-year-old Toot had only six months left to live, but for Obama it was never too late to brand someone you love as a racist.

"I can no more disown [Wright] than I can disown my white grandmother," said Obama in Philadelphia. This was the money line, the takeaway line. Obama professed to love Toot despite the fact that she "once confessed her fear of black men who passed her by on the street and who on more than one occasion has uttered racial or ethnic stereotypes that made me cringe."

Obama claims he told the Toot story in his 1995 memoir, *Dreams from My Father*, but there he told it a shade more honestly. The "diminutive" Toot had been shaken by an encounter with a large, aggressive panhandler. It was her virtue-signaling, deadbeat husband who volunteered to the adolescent Obama that the "real reason" Toot was so upset was because the panhandler was black. "And I just don't think that's right," Stanley Dunham was reported to have told his grandson, a creepy thing to do if true.[8] As to Toot's uttering of cringeworthy "racial or ethnic stereotypes," that was all new material, dredged up or fully imagined to save Obama's career.

Obama admits that "Favs," wunderkind speechwriter Jon Favreau, wrote the first draft. "It worked," Obama boasts. "The networks carried the speech live, and within twenty-four hours, more than one million people had watched it on the internet—a record at the time." Throughout Obama's career, like Ted Kennedy's, the networks were always ready to bail Obama out. To show he's not quite the cold, calculating fish he seems, Obama claims to have called Toot the night of the speech. "You know I'm proud of you, don't you?" she reportedly told him. "And it was only after I hung up," Obama alleges, "that I allowed myself to cry." Pass the hankie.

The media ate the speech up. MSNBC's Chris Matthews, who earlier in the campaign confessed that upon hearing Obama speak he "felt this thrill going up my leg," was sent a-tingling once again. Matthews called Obama's Philadelphia speech "worthy of Abraham Lincoln" and "the best speech ever given on race in this country."[9] Matthews was not an outlier. Media praise was universal.

At a minimum, the best speech on race should at least have been honest. This one wasn't. Despite Obama's request that Wright "lie low," the good reverend refused to. As a black friend of Obama summed up Wright's response, "He went full ghetto on their ass." During an appearance at the National Press Club, Wright publicly denounced America as racist, praised Louis Farrakhan, and claimed the US government invented AIDS.[10]

"I knew what I had to do," writes Obama. Forty days and forty nights after insisting he could never disown the man who married him and Michelle and baptized their daughters, Obama "unequivocally denounced and separated myself from Reverend Wright." If Obama's speech embracing Wright "worked," his statement disowning Wright merely "served its purpose."[11] That purpose was to keep his candidacy alive, nothing nobler than that.

A Real American

Forever uncertain of who he was, Obama resented the authenticity of others, no one more so than Sarah Palin. "A 'real American,'" he says of Palin in quotes as though he were quoting her (he's not; there's no citation), "and fantastically proud of it."[12] Palin did not intimidate Obama the way Reverend Wright did, but something about the attractive young Alaskan governor got under Obama's delicately thin skin.

In the early summer of 2008, a few friends and I spoke about John McCain's likely vice-presidential pick. In that none of us were enthused about McCain—few conservatives were—we all hoped he would choose someone to shore up his right flank. When asked for my choice, I said, "Sarah Palin." Uniformly, my friends said, "Who?" I explained why I liked Palin—young, good-looking, big family, pro-life, pro-gun, pro–small government. As Alaska governor, she took on the state's corrupt Republican establishment and beat it senseless. At the time, she was riding an 80 percent approval rating. "What's not to like?" I asked.

Later in the summer I got a call from one of these guys. "How did you know?" he asked.

"Know what?"

"Know McCain was going to pick Palin?"

I didn't know, just guessed. Actually, it was more of a hope than a guess. For a while that summer, McCain had been openly entertaining the idea of recycling Al Gore's running mate from 2000, Joe Lieberman.

I was scheduled to go to the Republican National Convention the week after Labor Day, the first one I had ever attended. Had McCain picked Lieberman, I would not have gone. I am not sure I would have voted for McCain. Many conservatives were *certain* they would not. A Lieberman pick would have spelled disaster for McCain and especially for down-ticket Republicans.

The choice of Palin lifted the spirits of everyone I met at the St. Paul convention site. McCain's speech on the convention's final night was pure anticlimax. The night before, Palin had captured the crowd's heart. She dazzled. Even Obama had to agree. "Palin was a born performer," he writes. "Her forty-five-minute speech at the Republican National Convention in early September was a masterpiece of folksy populism and well-aimed zingers."

Obama quotes one of the zingers. Palin had zoomed in on what Obama calls his "biggest mistake of the campaign." While Hillary was still viable, Obama had flown to San Francisco for a high-dollar fundraiser. One of the "latte-drinking, Prius-driving West Coast liberals" in attendance asked him why he thought working-class citizens in states like Pennsylvania chose to "vote against their interests and elect Republicans."[13]

Obama writes of those latte drinkers as though they were a class apart. As Obama made comically clear in Iowa a year earlier, they were not. Said he on the campaign trail in response to a question on rising grain prices, "Anybody gone into Whole Foods lately and see what they charge for arugula? I mean, they're charging *a lot of money* for this stuff."[14] At the time, there was no Whole Foods store in the entire state. Unfortunately, the gaffe known as *Arugula-gate* does not make the memoir. It would have added some welcome humor.

If there was ever a case of one arugula eater leading another, Obama's explaining rural Pennsylvanians to San Francisco metrosexuals had to be it. "It's not surprising," he said, "then that they get bitter, they cling to guns or religion or antipathy toward people who aren't like them, or anti-immigrant sentiment, or anti-trade sentiment as a way to explain their frustrations."

Obama is able to repeat this comment word-for-word because a freelance writer recorded it and quoted him in a *Huffington Post* blog. He then adds an aside that I confess to laughing out loud when I read it: "This is what separates even the most liberal writers from their conservative counterparts—the willingness to flay politicians on their own side."

In Obama's world, two plus two equals five. In 2016, the two most prominent conservative publications, the *Weekly Standard* and the *National Review*, as well as the editorial page of the *Wall Street Journal*, routinely and often savagely flayed Donald Trump. In 2020, by contrast, Big Media and Big Tech openly conspired to block negative reporting on the wobbly Biden campaign. Apparently, Obama knows his readers well enough to know that they rarely, if ever, think outside the bubble.

At the convention, Palin used her own humble roots to make her point. "In small towns," she said with a smile, "we don't quite know what to make of a candidate who lavishes praise on working people when they're listening, and then talks about how bitterly they cling to their religion and guns when those people aren't listening." Writes Obama, in perhaps the best line of the book, "Ouch."[15]

In *A Promised Land*, Obama all but admits he had been upstaged, and he had been. After the convention speech, Palin's favorability ratings were higher than McCain's or Obama's. She enjoyed an 89 percent approval rating among Republicans and even a 33 percent rating among Democrats.[16] Obama concedes that Palin energized the campaign and that she was new and different. Having feigned objectivity for a moment, he lets loose his inner bitter kitten.

For all of her "performative gifts," you see, Palin did not have what it took to be president. "What became abundantly clear as soon as Sarah Palin stepped into the spotlight was that on just about every subject relevant to governing the country she had absolutely no idea what the hell she was talking about."[17]

This is a nervy claim, a graceless one at that. A Republican who said this about a Democrat would have his Twitter account closed and his office stormed by a swarm of women in pink pussy hats. Plus, the claim is nonsense. Obama is only two years older than Palin. She had served six years as mayor of a city and a year as chair of Alaska's Oil and Gas Conservation Commission before Obama was elected to the US Senate. True, she had served as Alaska governor for not quite two years when McCain selected her, but Obama had served in the US Senate for only two years when he chose to run for *president.*

Upon his unwelcome entrance into the race, Hillary said about Obama what Obama was now saying about Palin. Mark Penn, Hillary Clinton's chief campaign strategist, summed up the Clinton messaging in a 2007 memo: "This is no time for rookies. No time for rhetoric. It is a time for experienced leadership that gets results."[18] Then too, Palin was not running for president. John McCain was, and he would live for another ten cantankerous years. Palin would have had plenty of time to learn on the job.

Once the Democrats realized what a threat Palin posed, they started chipping away at her. They had considerable help from their media allies. Katie Couric would win the Walter Cronkite award for revealing that Palin did not read the *New York Times* over her morning coffee. *Saturday Night Live*, under the pretense of humor, made Palin the butt of a running joke. After twelve years of media abuse, Obama obviously feels comfortable reinforcing the now well-established media narrative that Palin was a dolt. Unlike his Harvard Law degree self, sniffs Obama, Palin "bounced among five colleges before graduating with a journalism degree." He never said she couldn't spell "arugula," but he might as well have. (I had to look "arugula" up.)

Obama makes no specific reference, however, to Palin's debate with would-be vice president Joe Biden just a month after the convention. By this time, the sixty-five-year-old Biden had already served an obscene thirty-five years in the US Senate. For all his time in politics, when Biden first heard of McCain's VP pick, he said, "Who the hell is Sarah Palin?"[19] If I knew who Palin was, why didn't Biden?

Given Palin's presumed ignorance and Biden's experience, smart money had Biden running a Zamboni over the hockey mom from Nowheresville, Alaska. That didn't happen. The subhead from the UK *Telegraph* summed up the evening's unlikely outcome: "Opinion was split over who won the vice-presidential debate between the Republican Sarah Palin and the Democrat Joe Biden, after neither managed to land a knock-out blow."[20]

Even in retrospect, no media outlet has characterized the Biden-Palin debate the way CNN would report on Obama's first debate with Mitt Romney four years later: "The sheer panic Democrats felt in 2012 after Mitt Romney demolished Barack Obama at their first presidential debate in Denver can't be overstated."[21] Sarah Palin had a month to prepare. Obama had six years, and he was "demolished" by a RINO governor wearing funny underwear.

All these years later, Palin's performance holds up well. Although Palin lacked Biden's insider knowledge, she cleverly covered her weakness and played to her strengths, extrapolating from her own core values in a way that neither Biden nor Obama ever could (neither of them having much of any).

"Now you said recently that higher taxes or asking for higher taxes or paying higher taxes is patriotic," said Palin at one point. "In the middle class of America, which is where Todd and I have been all of our lives, that's not patriotic. Patriotic is saying, government, you know, you're not always the solution. In fact, too often you're the problem. So, government, lessen the tax burden on our families and get out of the way and let the private sector and our families grow and thrive and prosper."[22]

Knowing his fans have preserved the same media-warped perspective on Palin that he has, the superior Obama indulges in a churlish bit of condescension. "It didn't matter what the topic was or what form the question took," he writes, "the Alaskan governor appeared lost, stringing words together like a kid trying to bluff her way through a test for which she had failed to study."[23] As shall be seen, Obama knew more than a little about bluffing his way through school.

More troubling to Obama, Palin's "incoherence" did not seem to faze most Republicans. Then and now, I consider myself among the unfazed. Of the four major candidates in the race, Palin's political philosophy was the *most* coherent. She was also the only one of the four with executive

BARACK OBAMA'S PROMISED LAND

experience, the only who had ever applied her philosophy to real-life problems.

Speaking of incoherence, Obama expresses shock at those conservatives "who'd spent a year dismissing me as inexperienced, and who'd spent decades decrying affirmative action, the erosion of intellectual standards, and the debasement of Western culture at the hands of multiculturalists—suddenly shilling for Palin."[24] In an otherwise well-edited book, the logical thread in this sequence eludes even the attentive reader.

Obama's attack on Palin leaps off the page like a *cri de coeur*. Her very solidity—"She'd married her high school sweetheart, had five kids (including a teenage son about to be deployed to Iraq and a baby with Down syndrome), professed a conservative Christian faith, and enjoyed hunting moose and elk during her spare time"[25]—seems to provoke Obama's deepest insecurities. Unlike Palin, Obama's personal story has been, in his own words, "stitched together," and, as shall be seen, he is not necessarily the one who has done the stitching.

Obama closes the chapter on Palin with a Cassandra-like warning that he would have been well advised to heed himself. Writes he of her emergence: "It was, of course, a sign of things to come, a larger, darker reality in which partisan affiliation and political expedience would threaten to blot out everything—your previous positions; your stated principles; even what your own senses, your eyes and ears, told you to be true."[26]

Former Obama Secretary of Transportation, Ray LaHood, a Republican, thought Obama's own increasing partisanship helped make that reality darker. LaHood wrote in his snooze-inducing memoir, *Seeking Bipartisanship*, "As time passed, the president seemed to me to become more isolated, more insulated from those outside the in-group, less engaged with others."[27] In a *Politico* summary of the Obama years, Matt Latimer, a former Bush speechwriter, echoed LaHood's sentiments. Although he admits to having considered voting for Obama, Latimer concluded, "Washington is very much the same, if not worse, at the close of these long, bitter, brutal years. That's not all Obama's fault, to be sure. Maybe mostly not his fault. But it is in part. And it isn't what he promised to people like me."[28]

Latimer was writing at the beginning of 2016. He had no idea what Obama and his cronies had in store for the Republican nominee Donald Trump. Trump adviser Carter Page found out the hard way. I write this the day after Page filed his seventy-five-million-dollar lawsuit against Obama's co-conspirators in the Russia hoax. I suspect Page knows Obama's "darker reality" much better than Obama does.

The Crazies

For Obama, Sarah Palin is the ur-deplorable, the essence of all that is wrong with the America he had hoped to transform. As shall be seen, his cruel dismissal of Palin and people like her undermines many of the more substantial promises he has ever made. America first heard those promises sixteen years before the publication of *A Promised Land*. Obama, then still an Illinois state senator, made his debut on the national stage at the 2004 Democratic National Convention in Boston. The little-known Obama gave the keynote address. "We quickly settled on him," wrote presidential candidate John Kerry of Obama. "It was an easy decision—a clean slate, someone fresh who could articulate a new vision, someone who was unexpected."[29]

If Michelle relentlessly nagged her husband about his slovenliness—"He left wet towels on the bathroom floor, cups and glasses scattered about the house, and the toilet seat up"[30]—his white mentors saw in Obama something uniquely "clean." Joe Biden certainly did. In 2007, Biden served up his impressively artless rationale for Obama's emergence. Said the future president, "I mean, you got the first mainstream African-American who is articulate and bright and clean and a nice-looking guy. I mean, that's a storybook, man."[31] A Republican would have had to apologize for "articulate" and resign over "clean," but the media have long allowed Democrats a certain license in what they say, especially on racial matters.

In *A Promised Land*, Obama tells how he spent several days writing the convention speech in longhand on a legal pad, as was his custom. "At some point," he muses, "I remembered a phrase I'd heard once during a sermon by my pastor, Jeremiah Wright, one that captured this spirit. The audacity of hope."[32] Actually, Wright's phrase was "the audacity to hope," but that is one of the minor gaps in Obama's memory. The major one is his failure to recollect that little of what he said that night in Boston was true.

This is not to say that Obama "lied," a phrase used much too casually in regard to politicians, especially presidents. Lying implies intentional deception. The lying Obama did that night was largely to himself. In that speech, as in his memoir, his refusal to understand who he is, how he got to the White House, and what he failed to accomplish dazzles the knowing reader.

"Now even as we speak," said Obama in that night's most memorable phrase, "there are those who are preparing to divide us, the spin masters, the negative ad peddlers who embrace the politics of anything goes. Well, I say to them tonight, there is not a liberal America and a conservative America—there is the United States of America. There is not a Black America and a White America and Latino America and Asian America—there's the United States of America."[33]

Although one gets no sense of this in *A Promised Land*, Barack Obama would prove to be the most divisive president in recent American history. The words of Rev. Jeremiah Wright and other paranoid influencers infect his thinking more than he knows or at least more than he cares to admit. The "E pluribus unum, out of many, one" that Obama endorsed in his 2004 speech warred throughout his presidency with Wright's "U.S. of KKK A" before finally surrendering.

A Promised Land subverts many of the 2004 speech's loftier aspirations, none more nakedly than the bromide, "There is not a liberal America and a conservative America." Although Obama does not use Hillary Clinton's pet phrase "deplorables" to describe conservatives, he might as well have. With one notable exception, *all* references to conservatives, at home and abroad, are pejorative.

His likeminded book reviewers fail to notice the animus. In the main, they think Obama too kind to the opposition, too willing to see all sides of an issue. "And so he is lavish with forgiveness and with praise," writes Chimamanda Ngozi Adichie in the *New York Times*, "giving the benefit of the doubt even to those barely deserving."[34]

For someone who has traveled to as many states as Obama—fifty-seven at last count—he shows remarkably little understanding of the citizens of at least fifty of those states. I offer my own understanding as a corrective. I was thirteen when Obama was born at some point in 1961—more on the exact date later. If there had been a JFK fan club in my heavily Catholic Newark, New Jersey, neighborhood, I would have been its president. I was that rabid, that tribal.

My allegiance to the Kennedys remained strong until Bobby's assassination in 1968. With his death I could no longer ignore the increasingly obvious contempt shown by the Democratic Party and its media allies for the working-class whites left behind in the nation's collapsing inner cities. In 1969, Ted Kennedy enshrined that contempt at Chappaquiddick. When he abandoned Mary Jo, I abandoned his party. The Kopechne family had lived in our housing project.

Among baby boom conservatives, probably half or more started their political lives as Democrats. We have not arrived at our current positions casually. We've had to reason our way to a workable political philosophy against the prevailing media-educational grain, which is why conservatives *always* outscore liberals and especially "moderates" on political knowledge tests.

For five years in the late 1990s I did a daily talk radio show in the Kansas City studio Rush Limbaugh once called home. In fact, our show aired in the two hours leading up to his show on his station. As anyone who has done talk radio will affirm, no one has ever done it better than Rush. I learned a lot from the callers—cops calling from patrol cars, truckers calling from trucks, farmers calling from combines. Given that the show had a left-right format, I also learned how the other side thought—or chose not to.

When the internet arrived, I was able to start writing books. In support of those books, I spoke to conservative groups from San Francisco—a surprisingly cool Tea Party there—to Long Island's Suffolk County. Over time, I developed a good understanding of how beyond-the-beltway conservatives think. I have communicated with thousands of them. In all that time, I might add, I never spoke to anyone who advocated anything like white supremacy, a recent addition to the Left's arsenal of slurs. Obama does not have a clue about these people, but that does not stop him and the book reviewers from believing he does.

When Obama first came to Washington in 2005, he may have aspired to find common ground with his peers across the aisle, especially if they were "cut from the same cloth" as the Republicans he knew while a state senator in Springfield. These, after all, were "regular guys who didn't stray from the party line or the lobbyists who kept them in power but who also didn't consider politics a blood sport and might even work with you if it didn't cost them too much politically."[35]

From the conservative perspective, several of the Republicans Obama met in Washington seemed cut from the same cloth as the Republicans in Springfield. These included John Boehner, the House Minority Leader when Obama became president in 2008 and the Speaker of the House for two terms during Obama's presidency. "Boehner was a different animal," Obama writes, "an affable, gravel-voiced son of a bartender from outside Cincinnati."[36]

In *A Promised Land*, Obama describes each major player as a novelist might, both in terms of appearance and of character. Republicans are usually lacking in both. Despite his "human qualities," Boehner failed to live up to Obama's limited expectations because of "his tenuous grip on his caucus." By "caucus," Obama means actual conservatives who believe in things—most of those things being, in his view, implicitly racist.

Boehner's amoral twin, the "short, owlish" Senate Leader Mitch McConnell, fares little better. Like Boehner, McConnell lacked "any strong convictions" save one, "almost religious opposition to any version of campaign finance reform."[37] These were the two men that would shepherd the forces against Obama during his presidency, invariably, as

Obama saw it, for the wrong reasons. He took neither of them seriously. Boehner graduated from Xavier University in Cincinnati, McConnell from the University of Louisville and the University of Kentucky College of Law. They were not in his league. I doubt if, to this day, Obama knows that McConnell attended the 1963 March on Washington (among other civil rights rallies), not necessarily a CV enhancer for a would-be Kentucky politician.

Two other Republicans who play feature roles in *A Promised Land* are often paired: Senators John McCain and Lindsey Graham. The reader is warned to distrust Graham from the get-go. One can expect nothing but treachery from a man who is "short in stature, with a puggish face and a gentle southern drawl that in an instant could flip from warm to menacing." Given his "adoration" of McCain, the "unscrupulous" Graham occasionally lined up on Obama's side of an issue, but Obama "wasn't wild about having to depend on" him.[38]

For Obama, again with one exception, the only good Republican is a dead Republican. McCain fares better than any Republican other than Abraham Lincoln. Obama claims to have admired his courage as a navy pilot, but what he really appreciated was McCain's "contrarian sensibility and willingness to buck Republican Party orthodoxy on climate change and immigration."[39] In fact, McCain's primary role in Obama's memoir is to shed light on "the race-tinged nativism that regularly infected other Republican politicians."[40] McCain was above all this. "He wasn't an ideologue," says Obama, which is his way of complimenting McCain for not believing in much of anything.

The same president who rode to office promising there was no liberal America and no conservative America uses McCain as a vehicle to trash conservative America. "John had confided to me that he couldn't stand a lot of the 'crazies' in his own party," writes Obama, adding the complimentary sidebar, "The disdain he expressed for the far-right wing of his party wasn't an act."[41] In fact, Obama so reflexively uses the word "crazies" to describe the "far-right wing" that he carelessly repeats the slur a page later.

In American politics, Obama's readers quickly learn, there are only two "wings:" the "right wing" and the "West Wing." There is not a single reference to an American left wing, let alone a far-left wing. Nor do we hear of any American socialists. For him "socialist" is an empty accusation leveled by the crazies, as in, "I was also a secret Muslim socialist, a Manchurian candidate,"[42] or, "[Joe the Plumber] had unmasked my secret, socialist income-redistribution agenda."[43]

Obama even rejects the label "progressive" to describe his political philosophy. Obama sees progressives as less extreme than the "crazies," but he imagines them the way President Kennedy imagined "liberals," uneasy allies at best, self-righteous prigs at worst. In *A Promised Land*, they stand outside his inner circle prodding him unreflectively to the left. He writes, for instance, of "progressives unhappy that we hadn't done more to remake the banks" and of progressives with their "impractical demands." The one label he seems most comfortable with is "liberal," but even this word sometimes makes him squirm. The one label Obama does reject is "centrist," a label he identifies with the "triangulating, Davos-attending, Wall Street-coddling, Washington-focused" presidency of Bill Clinton.[44]

This uncertainty speaks to the question of who Obama really is, a question he never quite addresses because he may not know the answer. In July 2010, for instance, he confronted outspoken black professor Cornel West at the 2010 National Urban League Convention. Frustrated by West's taunting from the left, he came down to West's seat and hissed within earshot of others, "I'm not progressive? What kind of shit is this?"[45] Obama's account of this well-documented confrontation would have made good reading. Too bad he doesn't share it.

After nearly two decades of national exposure, Obama continues to remind us a little too much of Woody Allen's Zelig, a character Vincent Canby of the *New York Times* described as "so pathologically nil that, over the years, he has developed the unconscious ability to transform himself, physically and mentally, into the image of whatever strong personality he's with."[46]

Spooked by a Black Man in the White House

To this day, mainstream journalists know less about Obama's origins than they know about George Washington's. I wish I were exaggerating. I am not. Most journalists, perhaps all, could tell you where George Washington spent the first year of the life. Most, the great majority could *not* tell you where Obama spent his. Doubt me? Ask a journalist. More on this later.

Those hoping for some clarification about Obama's origins will not find it in *A Promised Land*. The book only muddies the water. If candidate Palin was a "real American" then candidate Obama was an unreal one. Former girlfriend Genevieve Cook certainly thought so. She lumped Obama among internationalists like herself, "people who spent their lives from the time they were born moving around from country to country, who are not members of any one culture, who come from nowhere in particular, and who do not really belong anywhere."[47]

More significantly, Hillary Clinton strategist Mark Penn came to a similar conclusion. "All of these articles about his boyhood in Indonesia and his life in Hawaii are geared toward showing [Obama's] background is diverse, multicultural and putting that in a new light," Penn wrote in a March 2007 memo to Hillary. "It also exposes a very strong weakness for him—his roots to basic American values and culture are at best limited.

I cannot imagine America electing a president during a time of war who is not at his center fundamentally American in his thinking and in his values."[48]

Of course, the Hillary campaign insisted it never attempted to follow Penn's lead, but Penn never suggested it should. "We are never going to say anything about his background," he added. "We have to show the value of ours when it comes to making decisions, understanding the needs of most Americans—the invisible Americans."

Attorney Philip Berg took his doubts about Obama a step further. On August 21, 2008, a week prior to the Democratic National Convention, Berg filed a federal suit in the Eastern District of Pennsylvania challenging Obama's constitutional eligibility to be president. A former deputy attorney general for the State of Pennsylvania and a credible pro-choice gubernatorial candidate in a Democratic primary against sitting governor Robert Casey, Berg expected to be taken seriously. He wasn't. The media expressed zero interest in his suit.

Obama and the Democratic National Committee (DNC), however, took a good deal of interest. Defending Obama was Bob Bauer, a top gun from the Deep State's go-to law firm, Perkins Coie. Bauer served as general counsel to the DNC and as personal lawyer to Obama during the 2008 campaign. In that capacity he led the legal fight against Berg. On November 12, 2009, the United States Court of Appeals, Third Circuit, ruled that Berg lacked standing to bring the suit.[49] The day after the suit was dismissed, the *New York Times* reported that White House counsel, Gregory B. Craig, was stepping down from his job. An anonymous source told the *Times* that Bauer would be taking over, and the source knew whereof he spoke.

With the media averting their collective gaze, a federal judge felt free to dismiss Berg's narrowly tailored suit without a hearing. "I was deprived of my due process rights to be heard," Berg would later write. "Judge Surrick made some outlandish comments claiming Obama had been properly vetted, and that was completely untrue."[50] Berg's claim here is accurate. The media's failure to investigate Obama's background is a scandal in its own right. (By the way, for those journalists who still may not know, Obama spent his first year in the one state named after George Washington. No, not Georgia.)

Berg would file additional suits, as would others. He simply requested to see some basic information about Obama, most notably his passport applications and his birth certificate. With little in the way of explanation, Obama's attorneys resisted at every turn. These attorneys included not only Bauer and other private attorneys, but also US Attorney General Eric Holder. "What a tragedy," writes Berg, "that our government with an opportunity to resolve this issue one way or the other, did not do so to protect Obama."[51]

Although a Hillary supporter, there is no reason to believe Berg was litigating on her behalf. He did not file his suit until well after the primaries had been settled, nor was Berg a Republican pawn. "Everyone says it was and is a right wing conspiracy against Obama," says Berg. "Well, I blow that theory out the door because I have been and still am a lifelong Democrat."[52] If Berg were a racist, his lifetime membership in the NAACP made for good cover. He argues that his primary goal in challenging Obama was to defend the Constitution. There is no reason to disbelieve him.

Obama does not mention Berg in *A Promised Land*. He does not have to. He is writing for an audience that has no idea who Berg is and that thinks of the word "birther" as a synonym for white supremacist. And birtherism would remain in the shadows until Donald Trump cast some light on the issue, beginning with his speech at the Conservative Political Action Committee (CPAC) convention in February 2011. "Our current president came out of nowhere, came out of nowhere," said Trump. "In fact I'll go a step further. The people who went to school with him, they never saw him; they don't know who he is. It's crazy." This is the only section of Trump's speech Obama quotes in *A Promised Land,* and it was largely improvised.

Obama omits what Trump said immediately afterward. "With no track record, and I will tell you, he's got nothing to criticize—you've got no record, you can't be criticized," Trump continued. "Wonderful guy, he's a nice man, but there was no record, nothing to criticize. He didn't go in wars, he didn't go in battles, he didn't beat this one, that one, have enemies all over the place. Nobody knew who the hell he was. He's now our president; he's our president. But he is our president."

In *A Promised Land*, Obama takes undue offense at Trump's speech, and he invokes the hockey mom's specter to do so. "I'd noticed," he writes, "how the mood we'd first witnessed in the fading days of Sarah Palin's campaign rallies and on through the Tea Party summer had migrated from the fringe of GOP politics to the center—an emotional, almost visceral, reaction to my presidency." No, what is visceral here is Obama's paranoia. "It was as if my very presence in the White House had triggered a deep-seated panic, a sense that the natural order had been disrupted." Not since Richard Nixon has a president worried so much about so little.

Having attended this particular CPAC, the only one I ever did attend, I can assure Mr. Obama there was no panic. Most of the attendees were under thirty. They were there to have a good time. More than a few were staying at the same off-brand hotel that I was, about a half-mile from the convention site. As I walked through my dreary hotel lobby one morning, I spotted a dead ringer for Sarah Palin. Once outside, a couple young guys approached me and asked if I thought the woman in the trademark red suit was Palin. "That woman is staying at our eighty-five-dollar-a-night hotel," I smiled. "What do you think?" I saw the woman later in the convention center lobby. Surrounded by a horde of young men, she was signing their programs, "Sarah Palin." The lady did a better impersonation than Tina Fey.

Recalling this moment at the hotel, I am struck anew by Obama's fixation on Palin as a Sarah the un-Baptist to Trump's anti-Christ. "Through Palin," he observes, "it seemed as if the dark spirits that had long been lurking on the edges of the modern Republican Party—xenophobia, anti-intellectualism, paranoid conspiracy theories, an antipathy toward Black and brown folks—were finding their way to center stage."[53] Obama conjures these infernal images unaware of how certifiably deranged he sounds.

He may have read too much Stephen Glass. Glass memorably documented the shenanigans of the CPAC crowd in a now famous *New Republic* article titled "Spring Breakdown." Glass set the scene at Washington's Omni Shoreham Hotel in 1997. Eight young men sit facing each other in a hotel room, passing a joint and making plans "in between rantings about feminists, gays and political correctness." The plan is for three of the men to go to a local bar, pick up "the ugliest and loneliest woman they can find," and have one of the men bring "the whale" back to the hotel room. "The five who stay behind," writes Glass, "will hide under the beds. After Seth undresses the whale, the five will jump out and shout, 'We're beaching! Whale spotted!' They will take a photograph of the unfortunate woman."

Writes Glass in the way of summary, "This is the face of young conservatism in 1997: pissed off and pissed; dejected, depressed, drunk and dumb."[54] Glass was writing for the same audience for which Obama writes. So blinded are these readers by their contempt, there is almost no evil they are unwilling to impute to conservatives, from white supremacy to fat-shaming. Glass went another year writing this gothic malarkey for the *New Republic* as well as *Policy Review, George, Rolling Stone*, and *Harper's* before getting busted. The *New Republic* conceded that at least twenty-seven of the forty-one articles that Glass wrote for the magazine had been fabricated. As shall be seen, Obama's fabrications are subtler but much more dangerous.

Trump said so little about Obama at the 2011 CPAC that it is hard to understand what made Obama feel the need to remind his readers of the speech. Trump did not come to CPAC to insult Obama but to dangle the idea of a presidential run. "While I'm not at this time a candidate for the presidency," Trump told the youthful crowd. "I will decide by June whether or not I will become one."[55] Trump was explaining why so few business leaders aspired to the presidency. "The fact is, this theory of a very successful person running for office is rarely tested because most successful people don't want to be scrutinized or abused," he said prophetically. "And that's what happens. If you see it, that's what happens. And this is why we don't have the kind of people that we should have running for office.["]56 Trump served up Obama's largely inconsequential background as a point of contrast.

As Obama sees it, with the CPAC speech Trump began to exploit the "panic" on the right by "peddling assertions that I had not been born in the United States and was thus an illegitimate president." In what may be his memoir's single most offensive sentence, Obama adds, "For millions of Americans spooked by a Black man in the White House, [Trump] promised an elixir for their racial anxiety."57 With all the skilled editorial eyeballs reviewing every line in numerous drafts, how is it, one wonders, how it is that no one flagged "spooked"? No, Obama had to have insisted on this racially loaded word, his impish thumb in the eye of an unworthy America.

Rather than speak for "the millions of Americans" allegedly unnerved by Obama's presence in the White House, I will speak for the one hundred thirty thousand residents of Chautauqua County, a semi-rural, rust belt paradise tucked away in the far southwest corner of western New York. I know the county well. Having spent a good chunk of each summer there, I used it as a backdrop for my first novel, *2006: The Chautauqua Rising*. In 2008, Obama *won* Chautauqua County. Chautauqua is only 2 percent black; many residents have not seen an African American in the county since the Buffalo Bills moved their training camp. "Racial anxiety" is preposterously low on the list of local motivators.

High on the list of real anxieties was the economy. The once prosperous county had been hemorrhaging jobs and people since 1970. In 2008, with the economy collapsing, Obama promised "hope and change." From the locals' perspective, he failed to deliver. In 2016, the county that Obama carried in 2008 gave Trump a twenty-two-point margin over the very white Hillary Clinton. Not even the good ladies of Code Pink could possibly believe that Hillary's sex caused more "panic" than Obama's race.

I Have Never Learned to Sail

"**I** turned to Rattner and Bloom and told them to get Chrysler on the phone," writes Obama as though he were scripting dialogue for a *Wall Street* sequel. Indeed, to read his account of the 2009 bailout of Chrysler and General Motors, one would think that he bailed out failing car companies for a living, so assured and competent does he seem. My personal favorite sentence is this: "If, with our help, the company could negotiate a deal with Fiat, I said, and deliver a realistic, hardheaded business plan to emerge from a structured bankruptcy within a reasonable time frame, we owed those workers and their communities that chance."[58] Even I get a tingle up my leg reading such manly dialogue.

In the course of his discussion on the bailout, Obama reveals a detail about his own life that undermines much of his posturing about race and class. "You know, it just so happens my first car was a '76 Fiat," Obama tells his colleagues during these negotiations. "Bought it used, my freshman year of college. Red, five-speed stick."[59] It wasn't *that* used. Obama started college in 1979.

As the purchase suggests, Obama lived a privileged life. I cannot imagine too many other black eighteen-year-olds in LA buying Fiats, even used ones. Some of Obama's privilege derives from his having grown up as a virtual only child in a financially comfortable white household. In 1970, as a fifth-grader, he enrolled in Punahou, Hawaii's most exclusive prep school. As biographer David Garrow reports, both his mother and stepfather were well paid at the time, and his grandmother had just been made a vice president of the Bank of Hawaii. His grandfather was also still working. Obama did not need or receive any financial aid.

This is not a reality with which Obama is comfortable. In *A Promised Land*, as elsewhere, he feels the need to impoverish his own background. Politicians have been doing this since Whig pols chose a log cabin as logo for the affluent William Henry Harrison. More recently, the ever-inventive Joe Biden purloined tales of evening football games after twelve-hour shifts in Welsh coal mines. Harrison and Biden, however, were not the beneficiaries of affirmative action. Obama has been. This makes his need to finesse the past more complicated than it is for a white office-seeker. And so, Obama tells the reader, "Despite having grown up in Hawaii, I have never learned to sail a boat; it wasn't a pastime my family could afford."[60]

That sentence is pure Obama, self-pitying and subtly anti-American. I say this from experience. At nineteen, I was the sailing instructor at a camp for inner-city *orphans*, almost all of them "of color," and these kids learned to sail. At the time I was living in a Newark housing project with my widowed mother, but I had learned to sail at fifteen while working as a dishwasher at a YMCA camp. And this was New Jersey, not Hawaii.

By the time Obama started at Punahou, the affirmative action imperium ruled all of academia. In 1965, when I was a senior in high school, my friend Albert and I were comparing notes. I told him how my guidance counselor laughed when I said I wanted to go to Princeton: "How are you going to afford that?" the counselor asked. Good question. I couldn't.

Albert sheepishly admitted he was going to Columbia. "How did you pull that off?" I asked. "A Negro deal," he said, embarrassed. Although a smart kid, Albert knew I had the better grades and scores. Plus, he was the richest kid in our grade school class ("rich" being a highly relative concept in our shabby Newark neighborhood). Obama would also go to Columbia, Michelle to Princeton. I went to an obscure Catholic college in upstate New York. In my *senior* year, I took out a student loan and

BARACK OBAMA'S PROMISED LAND

bought my first car: a used VW bug. Not complaining here, I was thrilled to have it. Only in America!

In 1975, when Obama was starting his high school years, I was finishing up my PhD at Purdue. So was my wife. During that year's hiring convention for modern languages, my wife and I bused in from Newark for her job interviews. After escorting her to a suite high up in some midtown Manhattan hotel, I took the elevator down to the lobby. On it, when I entered, were a young black male and a young white female. They were comparing the job interviews they had lined up. She had eight. He had fourteen. Together, all the white males in my department had zero. By the time we reached the lobby, I was rethinking my future.

It would not be in academia. The die there was well and fully cast. I never really wanted to be a professor anyhow. Happily, I was married to a woman. She had options. Had I been gay, I would have been doubly screwed. "Gay" was not yet a "metric." It soon enough would be.

As it happened, one of my male friends at Purdue did finally secure an interview. His wife wasn't thrilled at the prospect of moving to Cedar City, an isolated town of thirty thousand souls tucked away in southwest Utah, but a job was a job. Dennis flew out on his own dime. The SUU staff really liked him and would have hired him but felt pressured to give the job to a person of color, even if that person was from a foreign country, affirmative action and all. Sorry, Dennis. My friend retooled and went to law school.

The college Obama attended, Occidental, has long been among the most expensive in the country. In the most recent school year, tuition alone was more than fifty-six thousand dollars. Despite middling grades in high school, Obama started at Occidental on a full scholarship. For all his good efforts, Garrow has a hard time making sense of the conflicting accounts of what the scholarship entailed or how it came to be. In any case, Obama was able to afford a car, and none of his classmates can recall him holding a job.[61] It is hard to believe that Obama's race did not factor into his scholarship.

Throughout his adult life, and certainly in *A Promised Land*, Obama has had trouble determining how exactly he should present himself in regard to both race and class. As a consequence, he has always been uneasy about affirmative action and its opponents, especially given that his own circumstances undermine the historic rationale for affirmative action's existence.

"Accepting that African Americans and other minority groups might need extra help from the government—that their specific hardships could be traced to a brutal history of discrimination rather than immutable characteristics or individual choices—required a level of empathy, of fellow feeling, that many white voters found difficult to muster,"[62] Obama dares to write in *A Promised Land*.

Obama did nothing to deserve empathy at any level. He suffered neither hardship nor a brutal history of discrimination. His is a textbook case of why people of all races react to affirmative action—and its "diversity" mutation—with what he calls "open hostility." Not learning to sail scarcely merits a trip to Columbia and Harvard.

Even friendly biographers such as David Remnick and David Maraniss have a hard time taking Obama's own personal accounts of racial oppression seriously. Remnick admits that many of the grievances Obama cites in *Dreams from My Father* are "novelistic contrivances." If Obama "darkens the canvas" to score a racial point, writes Remnick, he does so because he is going "after an emotional truth."[63] In the real world, one cannot lie his way to a truth, emotional or otherwise. In *A Promised Land*, Obama continues to darken his own personal canvas. He never once, for instance, refers to himself as "biracial."

After two years at Occidental, Obama transferred to Columbia University, my friend Albert's alma mater. Obama finished Columbia in 1983. I have seen the graduation brochure. Contrary to rumor, he did graduate but not with honors. Remnick tells us that Obama was an "unspectacular" student in his two years at Columbia and at every educational venture before that going back to grade school.[64]

In *A Promised Land*, Obama whines, "Trump was on Fox so much that he soon felt obliged to throw in some fresh material, saying that there was something fishy about my getting into Harvard, given that my 'marks were lousy.'"[65]

By Harvard Law standards his marks were lousy. Applicants to Harvard Law typically have LSAT scores in the 98 to 99 percent range and GPAs north of 3.80. Northwestern University professor John McKnight, Obama's Alinskyite mentor in Chicago, laughingly said in a recorded video, "I think he didn't do too well in college, right."[66] McKnight wrote Obama a reference letter anyhow. As to Obama's LSAT scores, we'll know Pennsylvania's real 2020 vote count before we learn those.

When it came time to choose his law school, however, Obama well understood how the race game was played. He tells the reader in *Dreams*, he settled on three possibilities: "Harvard, Yale, Stanford."[67] In a brief moment of weakness, when I contemplated law school, my thoughts turned to Rutgers, Seton Hall, and Albany Law. Obama, however, was not deluding himself. Harvard, he knew, was keener on his DNA than his GPA, let alone his LSAT. As fellow alum Elena Kagan would tell Obama biographer Remnick, "By the time Barack got to campus, in 1988, all the talk and the debates were shifting to race."[68]

Obama also had friends. During a March 2008 interview on a New York–area show called *Inside City Hall,* host Dominic Carter asked venerable black politico Percy Sutton if he knew Barack Obama. Sutton casually answered that he had been "introduced to him by a friend" twenty years prior. Without forethought, Sutton correctly aligned the contact with the date of Obama's application to Harvard.

Sutton described the friend, Dr. Khalid al-Mansour, as "the principal adviser to one of the world's richest men," namely Saudi Prince Al-Waleed bin Talal. According to Sutton, al-Mansour called and asked him to "please write a letter in support of [Obama]...a young man that has applied to Harvard." The well-connected Sutton followed through on the request. He had absolutely no reason to make this story up, but Big Media ducked this potential bombshell, as have Obama's biographers.

Here I speculate—repeat, *speculate*—but it is possible the Saudis may have intervened on Obama's behalf even earlier. In November 1979, Vernon Jarrett, a widely syndicated black columnist then with the *Chicago Tribune*, relayed a conversation he had with al-Mansour. "What about those rumored billions of dollars the oil-rich Arab nations are supposed to unload on American black leaders and minority institutions?" asked Jarrett. Al-Mansour assured him that this was "not just a rumor." According to Jarrett, al-Mansour had been encouraging Arab leaders to take a more active role in black America that included "giving financial help to disadvantaged students."[69]

What make this story worth considering are several curious points of intersection. Obama bought his '76 Fiat in the fall of 1979 as a freshman at Occidental, the same year as the al-Mansour interview. Vernon Jarrett was the protégé of Obama's Hawaii mentor, the capital "C" Communist, Frank Marshall Davis. Obama's closest White House advisor, Valerie Jarrett, married Vernon Jarrett's son. Small world. BuzzFeed interviewed al-Mansour. He suggested that Jarrett, then deceased, was a fabricator and that Sutton was senile. This was proof enough for BuzzFeed editor and Obama sycophant, Ben Smith.

In that Big Media fully ignored both legs of this story, Obama supporters remain oblivious. Nevertheless, Obama chooses to revive it, at least a version twisted just enough to make the Tea Party "crazies" seem even crazier. He writes, "I hadn't just been born in Kenya, the story went, but I was also a secret Muslim socialist, a Manchurian candidate who'd been groomed from childhood—and planted in the United States using falsified documents—to infiltrate the highest reaches of the American government."[70]

For history's sake, what would have been much more helpful is an honest recounting of how Obama and his staff reacted when the Sutton video surfaced in August 2008. Sutton was highly respected. In the video he appears perfectly competent. The revelation was a potential game changer, but the reader does not even know there was a game being played.

As to affirmative action, Michelle Obama's case is even more compelling, more tragic. Although she too grew up in a comfortable two-parent family, she exploited the benefits of a program designed for those who did not. "Told by counselors that her SAT scores and her grades weren't good enough for an Ivy League school," writes biographer Christopher Andersen, "Michelle applied to Princeton and Harvard anyway."[71]

Sympathetic biographer Liza Mundy writes, "Michelle frequently deplores the modern reliance on test scores, describing herself as a person who did not test well."[72] In *Becoming*, Michelle admits as much. Although diligent, she struggled to get A's at the public magnet school she attended. After reviewing her grades and test scores, her high school counselor reportedly told her she was not "Princeton material."[73]

An angry Michelle defied her guidance counselor and applied to Princeton anyhow. "And ultimately, I suppose that I did show that college counselor," she writes, "because six or seven months later, a letter arrived in our mailbox on Euclid Avenue, offering me admission to Princeton."[74] It was cruel of Princeton to admit Michelle. The Princeton experience could only intensify her insecurities. Once there, she admits, she hung out almost exclusively with other black students. She tells of encounters with white students who questioned why she was there. "These moments could be demoralizing," she writes, "even if I'm sure I was just imagining some of it. It planted a seed of doubt. Was I here merely as part of a social experiment?"[75]

As her writing bears out, the answer to that question is yes. Friendly biographer Mundy describes Michelle's senior thesis at Princeton as "dense and turgid." The not-so-friendly Christopher Hitchens observed, "To describe [the thesis] as hard to read would be a mistake; the thesis cannot be 'read' at all, in the strict sense of the verb. This is because it wasn't written in any known language."[76]

Hitchens exaggerated only a little. The following summary statement by Michelle captures the grandiose, if syntactically challenged, sweep of her project: "The study inquires about the respondents' motivations to benefit him/herself, and the following social groups: the family, the Black community, the White community, God and church, the U.S. society, the non-White races of the world, and the human species as a whole."

Without intending, Michelle produced a serious indictment of affirmative action, not just in her manifest lack of writing style, but also in her content.[77] "I have found that at Princeton no matter how liberal and open-minded some of my white professors and classmates try to be toward me," she wrote in her thesis, "I sometimes feel like a visitor on campus; as I really don't belong."

The design of the thesis may be a disaster, but the idea behind it had merit. To test her thesis that "Blacks may be more comfortable with Whites as a result of a greater amount of exposure to whites in an academic setting while at Princeton," Michelle sent a survey to several hundred black Princeton alumni. She succeeded in getting eighty-nine of them to respond. The survey is a stark exercise in black and white. Michelle never used the phrase "African-American" (it had apparently not fully entered the lexicon by 1985), nor did she retreat to phrases like "people of color" or "minority groups." In her Princeton, there were only black people and white people.

In fact, the results of the survey refuted the thesis that Michelle had presumed to be true. After Princeton, blacks were uneasier around whites than they had been before. On the question of general comfort, 13 percent of the respondents claimed to have been comfortable with whites before Princeton, 4 percent while at Princeton, and only 1 percent post-Princeton. Michelle had stumbled upon a seriously inconvenient truth. In *Becoming*, Michelle confirms the failure of Princeton's "social experiment." She writes, "I imagine that the administrators at Princeton didn't love the fact that students of color largely stuck together. The hope was that all of us would mingle in heterogeneous harmony, deepening the quality of student life across the board."[78]

Michelle was not among the 1 percent who benefitted from exposure to whites. In *Becoming*, she writes positively of her childhood in a mixed-race neighborhood and of her adolescence at her mixed-race high school. It was at Princeton that things went south. In her thesis she imagined herself going forward "on the periphery of society; never becoming a full participant." In a sense, she never let herself become one, even in the White House. Refusing to understand what happened to her at Princeton, Michelle "dutifully reached for the next rung, applying to the best law schools in the country."[79] Harvard Law admitted her for the same reason the school would later admit her husband. A friend who attended Harvard Law at the same time as Obama tells me that professors, upon recognizing the writing gap between students admitted on merit and those admitted by race, knew enough to finesse students like Michelle through.

Barack Obama navigated in the white world with more authority than Michelle. This was, after all, the world he knew. If he lacked the scores to get in Harvard, he was smart enough to get by once in. "That I ended up doing well there I attribute mostly to the fact that I was a few years older than my classmates," Obama writes in *A Promised Land*.[80] In his early book on Obama, the always-observant Shelby Steele, himself biracial, suggests a more likely reason for Obama's success: "Blacks like Obama, who show merit where mediocrity is expected, enjoy a kind of reverse stigma, a slightly inflated reputation for 'freshness' and excellence because they defy expectations."[81]

While still a student at Harvard Law, Obama was willing to acknowledge the breaks he had gotten, admitting in a letter to the *Harvard Law Record* that he "undoubtedly benefited from affirmative action programs during my academic career" and "may have benefited from the Law Review's affirmative action policy when I was selected to join the Review last year."

In *A Promised Land*, all such nuance is lost. "In my second year, I was elected the first Black head of the *Law Review*, which generated a bit of national press,"[82] writes Obama with false modesty, and that's the sum of it. Garrow goes into considerably more detail about Obama's election. First, he had to be accepted to the *Harvard Law Review,* a rite of passage made much easier when the *Law Review* introduced an affirmative action metric in 1981. Obama was not the strongest candidate for the president's position based on traditional standards, including editing skills and intellectual prowess, but he was smart enough, friendly enough, and black enough. The timing was right for Obama. The timing has always been right for Obama. Upon graduation from Harvard Law, he was deluged with job offers.[83]

It would have been much better for all concerned if Obama had reminded his upwardly aspiring black supporters that corporate America and academia are eager to hire people like themselves and have been for the last half century. Of late this eagerness has been shading into desperation. In *A Promised Land*, unfortunately, Obama denies the obvious. He ridicules the "reverse racism" argument and rejects the idea that minorities enjoy "an unfair advantage" in the marketplace. This argument, he insists, has "nothing to do with the facts."[84]

That argument has everything to do with the facts. Not even the most ardent Obama supporter can say with a straight face that the Obamas have advanced "without regard to their race, color, or national origin." The slights they have suffered due to race have been negligible and the benefits enormous. Nor are conservative turning the race argument "on its ear." They are merely asking that the fundamental promise of the 1964 Civil Rights Act be extended to all Americans as intended. What is maddening about Obama is that he knows this. As the first black president, he was uniquely positioned to share the good news about race in America. Unfortunately, he chose not to.

An Attention-Seeking
Real Estate Developer

As the readers of *A Promised Land* cannot help but notice, Donald Trump haunts Obama's imagination the way Kong did the natives' of Skull Island. As of 2011, Obama had never met Trump. In the very first sentence in which he introduces Trump, Obama plays the one card he will play ad nauseam throughout *A Promised Land*. Yes, you guessed it.

He relates how "an attention-seeking real estate developer," namely Trump, "ominously" took out full-page ads in New York newspapers—the *Times* included—asking for a return of the death penalty in New York State. What prompted Trump's outrage in 1989 was a highly publicized night of "wilding" in New York City's Central Park that saw several New Yorkers assaulted and robbed and one woman jogger brutally raped and left for dead. Fortunately, she survived.

Trump made only one mention of race in the ad. The sentence read, "Many New York families—White, Black, Hispanic, and Asian—have had to give up the pleasure of a leisurely stroll in the Park at dusk."[85] It is Obama who injects race, noting that those accused of the rape were "Black and Latino teens" and that the victim was a "white jogger." Obama notes too that the accused were later exonerated of the rape, which is technically true, but there is massive evidence that the five were out that night assaulting people, including the jogger in question. As the

New York Times reported days after the attack, "The youths who raped and savagely beat a young investment banker as she jogged in Central Park Wednesday night were part of a loosely organized gang of 32 schoolboys whose random, motiveless assaults terrorized at least eight other people over nearly two hours, senior police investigators said yesterday."[86]

In his nasty little sidebar, Obama fails to mention that Trump never called for the teens to get the death penalty. That was to be reserved for "murderers." In 1989, there were 2,246 murders in New York City, the fifth straight year the city had seen an increase. In 1989, Trump's op-ed ad barely made a stir. The fact that the *New York Times* published it suggests how close to the conventional wisdom were Trump's opinions. The *Times* reporting on the ad—"Angered by Attack, Trump Urges Return Of the Death Penalty"—was admirably nonjudgmental.[87]

Under Democratic mayor David Dinkins, the homicide rate continued to increase for the four years following the mass assault. So traumatized were New Yorkers that in 1993 they chose a Republican to be mayor. After Rudy Giuliani took office, the homicide rate began to plummet. Eight years later, there were fifteen hundred fewer murders than there had been in the year Giuliani was elected. The great majority of lives saved were black and Latino. As shall be seen, Obama, like many Democrats, is either ignorant of the effects of his words and actions on black lives or fully indifferent.

"Trump's sudden embrace of birtherism" in 2011 took Obama by surprise. At first, he claims to have paid no attention. As Obama saw things, his biography had been "exhaustively documented." His birth certificate was on file in Hawaii. His grandparents had saved a clipping of his birth announcement in the local newspaper. As a kid, he walked by the hospital where he had been born every day on his way to school.

Obama's nonchalance here is deceptive. By early 2011, he had been fighting lawsuits by Berg and others for three years. Obama had to have been aware of the measure taken by Army flight surgeon Lt. Col. Terry Lakin in 2010. When asked to show his birth certificate prior to deployment to Afghanistan, his second such deployment, Lakin requested that his commander-in-chief show his. He walked his request through every level of Army bureaucracy, right up to and including a court martial. Like Berg, Lakin was disallowed from making his case against Obama in open court. In December 2010, he was shipped off in chains to the United States Disciplinary Barracks at Fort Leavenworth, leaving his Thai wife and three biracial children a thousand miles behind.

Obama would like to think that media outlets "eagerly lined up to offer a platform for a baseless claim," but Lakin knows otherwise. He was the first military resister in decades whose cause the media did not champion. He could have changed his sex, and reporters still would have ignored him. Writ large, they took his and Trump's accusations no more seriously than Obama claims to.

The more respectable conservative media shied away from "bitherism" as well, even Breitbart. In May 2012 editor Joel Pollak prefaced a Breitbart article with this disclaimer, "Andrew Breitbart was never a 'Birther,' and Breitbart News is a site that has never advocated the narrative of 'Birtherism.' In fact, Andrew believed, as we do, that President Barack Obama was born in Honolulu, Hawaii, on August 4, 1961."[88]

What is curious about Pollak's disclaimer is that it preceded a bombshell "birther" revelation. Breitbart had just unearthed a 1991 brochure from Obama's literary agency claiming that Obama "was born in Kenya." Although agency execs would blame a "clerical error" twenty years prior, the claim collapsed under the slightest scrutiny. As a matter of course, authors provide their own bios. Obama/Zelig was likely trying to make his background sound more exotic, more international, less, well, African American.

The mystery surrounding Obama's birth might best be left behind were it not for his obsession with the people who have questioned it, most notably Trump. Obama argues that Trump jeopardized not only his reputation, but also the very safety of his family. "Trump didn't care about the consequences of spreading conspiracy theories that he almost certainly knew to be false, so long as it achieved his aims," Obama insists. And it was not just Trump. Boehner and McConnell were equally indifferent to the truth. "The only difference between Trump's style of politics and theirs was Trump's lack of inhibition."[89] Yet, the fact remains that it was

Obama and his acolytes who were spreading untruths about Obama's origins. Worse, they imputed racism to anyone who doubted them.

In that Trump made for good copy, he got some airtime here and there, more on Fox News than elsewhere. Fox's motives are clear to Obama, given that its "power and profits had been built around stoking the same racial fears and resentments that Trump now sought to exploit."[90] As the reader has noticed, Obama's response to even the mildest criticism has a Tourette's-like quality to it. What else could motivate his critics but race?

Hillary's pollster Mark Penn knew better. No one thought to challenge Jesse Jackson's citizenship when he ran for president in 1988 or Al Sharpton's when he made a stab at the same sixteen years later. They were every bit as "real" as Sarah Palin. Obama's vulnerability, said Penn, was that his "roots to basic American values and culture are at best limited."[91] His presidency proved that out.

I Didn't Know My Father

In *A Promised Land,* Obama attempts to shore up his American roots by killing off his international ones. This move took some thought. Obama wrote his first memoir, *Dreams from My Father,* about his Homeric quest for identity, a Telemachus searching for his own Odysseus, the Kenyan Barack Obama. Stunningly, in *A Promised Land,* the Kenyan is an afterthought. "Since I didn't know my father," writes Obama casually, "he didn't have much input."[92]

This lack of "input" will come as news to popular conservative author Dinesh D'Souza. In his bestseller *The Roots of Obama's Rage,* D'Souza argued that that the senior Barack Obama was "first and foremost" an anti-colonialist and that his son was too. Both assertions are arguably true. Essential to D'Souza's thesis was that Obama inherited the philosophy and its attendant rage from the father with whom he shared a home until the age of two. After his father's departure, his mother preserved and passed along the Kenyan's anti-colonial worldview.

Although I have dissented in the past from D'Souza's thesis, Obama left enough clues in *Dreams* and elsewhere to make that thesis viable. On any number of occasions, including in the pages of *Dreams,* Obama claimed his father left Hawaii in 1963, "when I was only two years old."[93] In a talk to America's schoolchildren in September 2009, Obama repeated the canard. "I get it," he told his coerced audience. "I know what that's like. My father left my family when I was two years old, and I was raised by a single mother."[94]

"It's no use going back to yesterday," Alice tells her friends in Wonderland, "because I was a different person then."[95] Obama seems to be telling his friends much the same thing in *A Promised Land*. This new memoir all but erases the Kenyan from Obama's history. Obama says he met his presumed father only once at age ten when the older Obama visited Honolulu. "That was the first and last I saw of him," writes Obama. The first? This is a stunning admission, one that mainstream reviewers chose not to notice. Obama *began* his 2004 convention speech talking about his father. After thanking everyone, Obama dedicated the next three paragraphs to the father who allegedly helped him become the man he became. As a loving couple Barack Obama and Stanley Ann Dunham made Obama's ascendancy possible.

"My parents shared not only an improbable love, they shared an abiding faith in the possibilities of this nation," said Obama. "They would give me an African name, Barack, or 'blessed,' believing that in a tolerant America your name is no barrier to success. They imagined me going to the best schools in the land, even though they weren't rich, because in a generous America you don't have to be rich to achieve your potential. They are both passed away now. And yet, I know that, on this night, they look down on me with great pride."[96] As Obama concedes in this new memoir, there was no "they." The 2017 publication of David Garrow's *Rising Star* may have cautioned Obama to stop repeating a story that observant people on the left now knew to be false.

Obama's living African relatives got an early preview of Obama's shape-shifting. The senior Barack Obama's oldest son, Malik, first met his half-brother in Washington in 1985, and the two became close. "I loved him unconditionally," Malik would tell filmmaker Joel Gilbert in 2015.[97] Barack would go on to serve as the best man at Malik's wedding, and Malik would serve as the best man at his. In fact, Obama closes *Dreams* with a detailed tribute to Malik, then called Abongo, at his and Michelle's wedding. "He looked so dignified in his black African gown with white trim and matching cap that some of our guests mistook him for my father," writes Obama in *Dreams*. "He was certainly the older brother that day."[98]

Yet in *A Promised Land*, Malik does not merit a single mention. On one occasion Obama speaks of "wearing an African outfit at my Kenyan half brother's wedding,"[99] but he cannot bring himself to say his brother's name. Obama mentions the photo only to complain how it was used to raise doubts about his citizenship. Malik's expulsion from Obama's mythology would not surprise him or other members of the African family. Although several of them attended Obama's 2009 inauguration, including Obama's Aunt Zeituni, Malik "didn't feel like we were actually welcome."

Zeituni, who lived in public housing in Boston, died in 2014 at age sixty-one. When Malik approached Obama for financial help to send Zeituni's body back to Kenya for burial, Obama turned him down. Malik was crushed. "I don't understand," Malik told filmmaker Gilbert, "how somebody who claims to be a relative or a brother can behave the way that he's behaving, can be so cold and ruthless, just turn his back on the people he said were his family."[100] There is no mention of Zeituni in *A Promised Land* either.

The Kenya fable was more useful to Obama than actual Kenyans. He built his candidacy on his African roots. According to friendly biographer David Remnick, Obama's "signature appeal" was just this: "the use of the details of his own life as a reflection of a kind of multicultural ideal."[101] And now in *A Promised Land*, Obama quietly concedes it was all a fable. There was no improbable love, no faith in the future of America, no family, no "they."

In purging his past, Obama went harder on "Frank" than he did on Malik or even on Obama Senior. In *Dreams*, he talks about Frank, as in Frank Marshall Davis, more than he does any nonfamily member. In *A Promised Land*, Obama mentions him not at all. A card-carrying member of the Communist Party USA, a bisexual libertine, and the author of a pornographic memoir only slightly more fictionalized than *Dreams*, Davis was a genuine character. As the man who introduced Obama to the perils of being black, he deserved attention. Obama gives him none.

For all the energy Obama spends rebuking those who question his past, he refuses to attack even filmmaker Joel Gilbert whose widely seen documentary *Dreams from My Real Father* argued that Davis was Obama's biological dad.

Given the widespread myopia of the American media, I suspect few American journalists even know who Davis is. Obama's biographers, however, have begun to acknowledge the role he played in Obama's life. In his sophomore year at Occidental, Obama even wrote a poem about "Pop." Knowing little of Obama's history, literary critics assumed the poem was about Obama's grandfather, Stanley Dunham, a man Obama called "Gramps." *New Yorker* reviewer Rebecca Mead, for instance, "called the poem a loving if slightly jaded portrait of Obama's maternal grandfather."[102]

Biographer David Maraniss and historian Paul Kengor have endorsed my early analysis that "Pop" is Davis. According to filmmaker Gilbert, who interviewed Obama school friend Keith Kakugawa, Obama's nickname for Davis was "Pop." Garrow knows my thesis is correct, but he cannot quite bring himself to say so. He writes, "But hostile critics focused on how the subject 'recites an old poem he wrote before his mother died' and noted that Stan's mother had killed herself when he was eight years old." In the footnotes, Garrow cites Kengor and me as the "hostile critics" in question. "Honest critics" would have been more accurate. I would bet my house against Garrow's mailbox that "Pop" is Davis. Garrow counters, "Barack would forcefully reject the Davis hypothesis," and quotes Obama as saying, "This is about my grandfather."[103]

Obama was lying. He was erasing Davis from his history. His purge began soon after his national debut at the 2004 Democratic National Convention. As Kengor has observed, Obama removed twenty-two references to Davis from the audio version of *Dreams* recorded in 2005.[104] Although Obama takes bitter delight in shooting down rumors about himself in *A Promised Land*, he leaves the Davis rumors alone. In fact, he does not mention Davis *at all*. That choice surprised me. Davis was too important, too useful to Obama's larger story about race to ignore. Calculation went into the decision to axe Pop. Those calculations will, I fear, be lost to history.

There Were Black Folks Who Heard It

To this day one speaks about the fraud at the core of Obama's candidacy at his peril. During the 2008 primary campaign, Bill Clinton found himself in hot water for using the term "fairy tale" in regard to Barack Obama. As Obama admits, Clinton was describing Obama's shallow opposition to the war in Iraq, but the race-baiters in Obama's camp pulled the phrase out of context to paint Clinton and, by extension, wife Hillary as racists. Writes Obama, "There were Black folks who heard it as a suggestion that the notion of me as president was a fairy tale."[105] Obama adds that South Carolina Congressman Jim Clyburn, at that time America's most powerful black leader, publicly rebuked Clinton over the remark.

Of course, Obama could have exonerated Clinton before the primary, but that would not have helped him secure the black vote. On Election Day, he received 80 percent of "a massive black turnout" and 24 percent of the white vote to win the primary easily. So convinced were black voters of the Clintons' racism that eight years later Bill Clinton, as the *Politico* headline affirms, felt the need to "seek redemption in South Carolina."[106]

Bill Clinton was, of course, righter than he knew. The story Obama told repeatedly on the campaign trail was a fairy tale. Pollster Mark Penn understood this. He privately labeled Obama a "phony." Penn wrote to Hillary in 2007, "He told the people of NH yesterday he has a Kansas accent because his mother was from there. His mother lived in many states as far as we can tell—but this is an example of the nonsense he uses to cover this up."[107]

Obama is still covering up for his mother. Throughout *A Promised Land,* the omissions often loom larger than the story told. One such omission is Seattle. Seattle, not Kansas, is where his mother spent her formative years. Seattle, not Hawaii, is where Obama spent the first year of his life. In fact, mother and son lived on Capitol Hill, just a few blocks outside the famed Capitol Hill Autonomous Zone, or CHAZ. Despite the city's importance to Obama's life story, there is no mention of "Seattle" in the memoir.

Obama's most serious biographers—the three Davids, all Pulitzer Prize winners: Remnick, Maraniss, and Garrow—report the Dunham family's move to Seattle in 1954 or 1955 when Ann was about twelve. There is little controversy here. Altogether less clear is why the Dunhams abruptly moved to Hawaii in 1960 when Ann was seventeen. Although the three biographers disagree on the details, they agree that Ann went unwillingly in the summer after her high school graduation. The putative reason for the move was a new opportunity for Stanley Dunham in the retail furniture business, but little is said of Toot, Madelyn Payne Dunham, Obama's grandmother. At the time of the family's departure, Madelyn was working as an escrow officer at a local bank. She promptly found a job in Honolulu doing much the same thing and worked her way up to become one of the bank's first female vice presidents.

In *A Promised Land*, Obama speaks of Toot glowingly. She was the earner in the family, the one willing "to carry the load in front of her"[108] to provide for Barack and Stanley, who had abandoned the furniture business by the time we meet him in *Dreams*. One suspects that Toot was no more enthused about the move to Hawaii than her daughter was, and yet she went, ostensibly so her Willy Loman of a husband could have one more shot at pursuing his humble dreams.

I think there may have been another reason, and here, I *speculate*. In high school, Ann proved to be something of a rebel—a liberal and wannabe beatnik who hung out at jazz bars and once even hit the road with a friend Kerouac-style. As Garrow reports, Ann saw the celebrated Franco-Brazilian film *Black Orpheus* while still in high school and "may have been especially struck by the film's male lead, black Brazilian actor Breno Mello."[109]

Obama speaks about his mother's reaction to this film at length in *Dreams*. In the summer before his senior year in college, Ann visited him in New York and dragged him to see *Black Orpheus* at a revival house. Obama was bored. Ann was not. She explained that she had first seen the film in the summer before her senior year in high school while working as an au pair in Chicago. "I thought it was the most beautiful thing I had ever seen," she tells her son.

Her enthusiasm embarrasses Obama. Imagining himself the arbiter of all things *noir*, he muses callously, "I suddenly realized that the depiction of childlike blacks I was now seeing on the screen, the reverse image of Conrad's dark savages, was what my mother had carried with her to Hawaii all those years before, a reflection of the simple fantasies that had been forbidden to a white middle-class girl from Kansas, the promise of another life: warm, sensual, exotic, different."

Obama underestimated his "Kansas" mother. She was not exactly Dorothy. The one possibility that makes the most sense of the facts surrounding Obama's birth is that she had a black lover on the mainland. In 1960, parents routinely sent their pregnant daughters to visit an "aunt" in some distant city before they started to show. In 1960, if the baby's father was black, a white mother-to-be could go no place more welcoming than Hawaii. There a biracial child had a decent chance of growing up without stigma.

In the official story, Ann meets Barack Obama in a Russian class. This much is likely true. Much more suspect is the notion that Obama falls in love with Ann. In this regard, Garrow is the most honest and unsparing of the biographers. He writes, "In truth, as one scholar would acutely put it, Barack Hussein Obama was only 'a sperm donor in his son's life.'"[110] Obama confirms as much when he admits he never saw the Kenyan Barack Obama before he was ten.

Barack Obama's official date of birth is August 4, 1961. Presuming a normal pregnancy, Ann would have conceived the child in early November, an estimated six weeks after starting class. Rebellious and infatuated with exotic men, she could have met and promptly seduced or been seduced by Obama. Just as likely, she and her father could have been on the lookout for someone willing to put his name on the birth certificate.

In 1961, Africans had higher status in America than African Americans. An African who wanted to have his student visa extended could see the merits in marrying a pregnant American girl even if he did have a wife back in Kenya. What cannot be denied is that Obama and Stanley Dunham became buddies. A photo captures them arm-in-arm when Obama leaves for Harvard a year and a half after he allegedly knocked up Dunham's underage daughter. One other variable: Ann does not enroll for the second semester at the University of Hawaii. If she were just a couple months pregnant there would be no reason not to. Mumus cover a lot of sins.

As Garrow notes, Ann and Barack reportedly flew to Maui on February 2, 1961, and were married there. He admits, however, that no contemporary documents have ever been located. Even less helpful is the account by Janny Scott, the *New York Times* reporter who spent two years researching her 2011 biography of Ann Dunham, *A Singular Woman*. Although Scott spends thirty pages documenting Ann's high school years in Seattle, she spends just two pages covering her courtship with Obama, the marriage, and birth.

On page eighty-four of the book, Scott writes, "Obama was twenty-four years old and Ann was seventeen when they met in the fall of 1960."[111] On page eighty-six, she tells the reader that baby Obama was born in Honolulu and "eleven months later, the elder Obama was gone." That's it.

As to the wedding itself, Scott can tell the reader no more than Garrow can. She also fails to comment on Ann Dunham's whereabouts from the day of the alleged wedding in February 1961 to Obama's reported birth in August 1961. Not a single word. There are no credible witnesses to any kind of relationship. There are no photos of a pregnant Ann or of a newborn Obama.

This brings us back to Obama's Seattle problem. In his 2012 biography Maraniss finally concedes what the alternative conservative media—the *samizdat* I call it in homage to the underground press in Soviet Russia—had first reported in 2008, namely that Ann Dunham emerged in Seattle with her baby in time to register at the University of Washington for the fall semester of 1961. "Within a month of the day Barry came home from the hospital," Maraniss writes of baby Obama, "he and his mother were long gone from Honolulu, back on the mainland, returned to the more familiar turf of Mercer Island and Seattle and the campus of the University of Washington."[112] Garrow acknowledges the same. Somehow, Obama's official campaign biography, Remnick's biography, Scott's bio of Ann Dunham, and Obama's *Dreams* all either botched the timeline or missed the Seattle sojourn altogether.

Parents who moved abruptly to Hawaii to protect their daughter's reputation would have had little compunction about registering a home birth six months after it actually happened, the final step in a well-executed plan to save face and give their grandson an identity. If my suspicions are right, the real issue may not be where Obama was born, but when. It's possible that Ann fled Hawaii in late August 1961 with a baby who was just a few weeks old, but her decision to leave would seem much more prudent if the baby had been born several months prior.

Until the time Obama ran for president, he may have believed the origins story his mother and grandparents fed him since childhood. He might not have learned the real story until after he declared for president. In any campaign, the candidate's staffers do a dumpster dive on their candidate to head off the opposition. Upon learning the truth, candidate Obama may have heard from his handlers what Senator Ranse Stoddard, Jimmy Stewart's character in *The Man Who Shot Liberty Valance*, heard from his: "This is the West, sir. When the legend becomes fact, print the legend." Once printed, that legend had to be protected. A birth date in January or February would have stripped Obama of what Remnick called his "signature appeal." More personally troubling, it would have deprived Obama of the very identity his mother and grandparents had labored to create.

To this day, not one reporter in a hundred knows that Obama spent the first year of his life in Seattle with his single mother. The widespread ignorance on this subject would not much matter save for the fact that Big Media, most prominent Democrats, and Obama himself still pillory Trump as a racist for questioning Obama's origins. By 2020, when his memoir was published, the Obamas had salted away their millions. They had nothing to worry about. Fabulation wasn't a crime. In an honest memoir, Obama could have told how he learned of the emptiness at the core of his family fable and why he persisted in sustaining it. But if your readers, even your reviewers, prefer the legend, I suppose there is not much incentive to print the facts.

A Guy Who Lives in
My Neighborhood

Chimamanda Ngozi Adichie begins her *New York Times* review of *A Promised Land* with this sentence, "Barack Obama is as fine a writer as they come."[113] This was, I am sure, music to Obama's ears. As one commenter on the *Washington Post* review deadpanned, "Obama may have been the first president, who became president, so he would have material for a memoir."[114]

Throughout his life, Obama has openly aspired to be a writer. He has forged his identity as much around being a man of letters as he has around being a man of politics. Indeed, it was the literary world's enthusiasm for what the *Times'* Jennifer Szalai called "Obama's extraordinary first book," *Dreams from My Father*, that fueled his political rise.[115]

A Promised Land was written to solidify that reputation. Considerable time and effort went into the book, much of that effort from others. Obama's long-time editor Rachel Klayman brought her "ferocious eye for detail to every line." Sara Corbett edited multiple drafts, "making critically helpful suggestions throughout." Speechwriter Cody Keenan contributed thoughtfully "in innumerable ways." Ben Rhodes "supplied key editorial and research support for each draft." And Samantha Power "offered rigorous, intelligent, and incredibly useful feedback through-out."[116] Several of these people are serious writers. Rhodes is an aspiring novelist. Corbett was the principal ghostwriter on Michelle's *Becoming*. Obama needed the book to read well, and it does. He could be confident that reviewers like Adichie would not factor the acknowledgments section into her assessment of Obama's literary gifts.

It obviously bugged Obama, however, that one person with a soapbox of consequence did not take those gifts seriously. In the spring of 2011, Trump emerged as Obama's skeptic-in-chief. Trump's critics have never let America forget his questioning of Obama's origins, but they have ignored Trump's questioning of Obama's literary chops. If the media were willing to let that challenge pass unnoticed, Obama's pride would not let him. As the Proverbs remind us, "Pride goeth before destruction, and an haughty spirit before a fall."

In Trump's search for "fresh material," writes Obama, "he told Laura Ingraham he was certain that Bill Ayers, my Chicago neighbor and former radical activist, was the true author of *Dreams from My Father*, since the book was too good to have been written by someone of my intellectual caliber."[117] Trump made the same claim on the Sean Hannity show.

"I heard he had terrible marks, and he ends up in Harvard," said Trump in his artless style. "He wrote a book that was better than Ernest Hemingway, but the second book was written by an average person."

"You suspect Bill Ayers?" said Hannity.

"I said, Bill Ayers wrote the book," Trump replied. He had previously made the claim in a public forum as well as on the Ingraham show. I have to take some credit for this exchange. In the spring of 2011 Trump's then attorney Michael Cohen called me out of the blue to ask what I knew about the birth certificate controversy. Knowing little at the time, I suggested that Cohen investigate the authorship issue. He apparently did. I have never, however, talked to Trump. Perhaps fearing Trump was right, Big Media refused to take the bait. Obama, to my surprise, did. He should not have. He has left himself vulnerable on two counts: his writing ability and his relationship with Bill Ayers.

Obama mentions Ayers just twice in the book: the instance referred to above and an earlier throwaway reference in which his "friendship with my neighbor Bill Ayers" is listed in a litany of dubious charges thrust at him by the likes of Sean Hannity and Rush Limbaugh during the 2008 campaign. Given Obama's detailed description of that campaign, he might usefully have spoken of the Ayers trap set for him by moderator and former Clinton adviser George Stephanopoulos during an April 2008 debate on ABC.

Speaking to the issue of "patriotism," Stephanopoulos asked Obama about his ties to Ayers. "He was part of the Weather Underground in the 1970s," said Stephanopoulos in setting up the question. "They bombed the Pentagon, the Capitol, and other buildings. He's never apologized for that." He then asked Obama, "Can you explain that relationship for the voters and explain to Democrats why it won't be a problem?" Left unsaid was that in Obama's neighborhood, Ayers's bombing of the Capitol made him something of a folk hero. Until January 6, 2021, progressives thought such an attack a cool thing.

This question followed one by Charles Gibson on why Obama did not wear a flag pin. In *A Promised Land*, Obama goes into some detail on the flag pin issue. Conservative talking heads, he writes with unusual vigor, "began to piss me off. Just why was it, I wanted to ask, that only my pin habits, and not those of any previous presidential candidates, had suddenly attracted so much attention?" He adds, "I told the truth, saying that I didn't think the presence or absence of a token you could buy in a dime store measured one's love of country."[118]

The "dime store" riff is new. During the 2008 debate Obama's answer on the flag pin question was much more circumspect, but the questioning of his patriotism visibly annoyed Obama, especially when it came from a Clinton crony. Although the Ayers question created a media firestorm, Obama does not discuss either the question or his memorable answer in *A Promised Land*.

"This is a guy who lives in my neighborhood, who's a professor of English in Chicago who I know and who I have not received some official endorsement from," snapped Obama at Stephanopoulos. "He's not somebody who I exchange ideas from on a regular basis." Much as he paired the Reverend Wright off with Toot, Obama linked neighbor Ayers and "his despicable acts" to Republican friend Sen. Tom Coburn, who "once said that it might be appropriate to apply the death penalty to those who carried out abortions." In his memoir, Obama describes Coburn as a "sincere and thoughtful friend." He is the only living Republican to win the president's approval, but Obama expresses no regret about comparing him to Ayers.[119] David Garrow spoke with Coburn about the slight. Coburn shrugged it off but wondered, "Why answer a question by throwing a friend under a bus?"[120]

For her part, Hillary thought the Ayers issue worth exploring. She reminded the audience that Obama had served in a paid directorship on the Woods Foundation with Ayers even after Ayers had said of his bombing campaign "that he was just sorry they hadn't done more."[121] Hillary did not get the quote exactly right, but she was close enough. In what Garrow calls "a horrible accident of timing," the *New York Times* review of Ayers's book *Fugitive Days* was published on September 11, 2001. The review began with the quote from Ayers, "I don't regret setting bombs. I feel we didn't do enough."

In reality, Ayers's involvement with Obama went much deeper than the Woods Foundation. If Obama mentions Ayers just twice in *A Promised Land*, Garrow mentions Ayers scores of times in his biography of Obama's early years, *Rising Star*. To repeat, Garrow is a Pulitzer Prize–winning civil rights historian and an exhaustive researcher. He interviewed Ayers and his terrorist bride, Bernardine Dohrn, as well many others in Obama's Chicago circle.

According to Garrow, Michelle's relationship with Dohrn dated back to their time together at the law firm, Sidley & Austin, in the late 1980s. During the early days of the Weather Underground, it was Dohrn, then something of a terrorist pinup, who was the public face of the organization. She was much better known than Ayers. They came together to Chicago from New York in 1987 with their children and quickly made friends with (among other people) Valerie Jarrett's parents, the Bowmans. In March 1995, Ayers used his influence to get Obama appointed as chair of the well-funded Chicago Annenberg Challenge. In September 1995, Ayers and Dohrn hosted a fundraiser for Obama's state senate campaign at their home.

"After that gathering," writes Garrow, "Barack and Michelle began to see a great deal more of not only Bill and Bernardine but also their three closest friends, Rashid and Mona Khalidi and Carole Travis." Garrow adds, "By the spring of 1996 Barack and Michelle were a regular presence at the two couples' 'very informal' dinners. 'I would invite them often,' Mona recounted. 'We used to do a lot of dinners together,' and 'they came to our house often.'"

Not until Obama's 2004 campaign for the US Senate did "Barack and Michelle's attendance at the almost nightly dinners at the Khalidis' or Bill Ayers and Bernardine Dohrn's home" begin to fall off.[122] As Garrow proves beyond doubt, Obama lied throughout the 2008 campaign about his relationship with Ayers and Dohrn. Ayers was much more than a "guy who lives in my neighborhood." He was an intimate friend. That revelation alone could have finished him in the primary.

The American Way
and All That Shit

As to Trump's accusation that Ayers was the true author of *Dreams,* Obama biographer David Remnick observed in 2010, "This was a charge that if ever proved true, or believed to be true among enough voters, could have been the end of the candidacy."[123]

I know something about this accusation, as I was the first one to level it. I stumbled on the Ayers-Obama controversy in the summer of 2008. I have written about this elsewhere so I will keep it brief. On first reading *Dreams,* I strongly suspected that Obama had help. The style of this 1995 memoir did not match his everyday expression or that of his prior literary efforts, which were minimal and amateurish. I harbored no suspicions about Ayers until I picked up *Fugitive Days* while following a separate thread and observed some striking parallels with *Dreams.* I went public with my thesis in late September 2008, which was promptly labeled racist by anyone on the left paying attention, including Remnick, Ta-Nehisi Coates, and comedian Bill Maher, among others.

As thorough a reporter as he is, David Garrow blinds himself to the research of those of us in the American samizdat. Without mentioning me by name, he dismisses my claim of Ayers's involvement as "far loony."[124] He works on the understanding that Ayers and Obama did not meet until February 1995, and by this time Obama's manuscript had already been sent to the publisher. He relies on the memory of his sources for this information, who, wittingly or otherwise, have misled him.

Recall that Michelle and Bernardine Dohrn worked together in the late 1980s. Ayers and Obama, I am convinced, were communicating no later than 1994 and, quite possibly, much earlier. The evidence for this earlier meeting can be found in *Dreams*. Unlike Obama, Bill Ayers has had a genuine, career-long interest in education. Critics of my thesis overlook the extraordinary mind meld between these secret sharers on that subject.

In his 1993 book, *To Teach*, Ayers makes a sharp distinction between education and training. "Education is for self-activating explorers of life, for those who would challenge fate, for doers and activists, for citizens," he writes. "Training," on the other hand, "is for slaves, for loyal subjects, for tractable employees, for willing consumers, for obedient soldiers." Adds Ayers, "What we call education is usually no more than training. We are so busy operating schools that we have lost sight of learning."

In *Dreams*, written two years later, these exact sentiments find colloquial expression in the person of Frank Marshall Davis, or "Frank" as he is known. "Understand something, boy," Frank tells the college-bound Obama. "You're not going to college to get educated. You're going there to get trained." Frank shares Ayers's ideological contempt for training. "They'll train you to forget what it is that you already know," Frank tells Obama. "They'll train you so good, you'll start believing what they tell you about equal opportunity and the American way and all that shit."

It gets better. In 1994, Ayers coauthored an article whose title befits a former merchant seaman: "Navigating a restless sea: The continuing struggle to achieve a decent education for African American youngsters in Chicago." In the mid-1990s, I believe his passion for reform inspired Ayers to engineer Obama's rise. As an African American, Obama could help Ayers chart a course he could not do on his own.

In "Navigating," Ayers and white coauthor Mike Klonsky lay out a detailed analysis of the Chicago school system and a discussion of potential reforms. Obama, despite an expressed lack of interest in educational issues, does much the same in *Dreams*. Curiously, he and Ayers have all but identical visions.

This cannot be a coincidence. "Navigating" and *Dreams* were written largely in the same year, 1994. Ayers was the dominant author of "Navigating" and likely the muse behind *Dreams*. Either Ayers helped Obama with *Dreams* or Obama lifted Ayers's ideas almost verbatim.

Celebrity biographer Christopher Andersen argues for the former in *Barack and Michelle: Portrait of an American Marriage*, a flattering bestseller about the first couple published in 2009. Andersen, in fact, zeroes in on the education connection. "What did interest Barack were Ayers's proven abilities as a writer," observes Andersen. "Ayers had written and co-written scores of articles and treatises, as well as several nonfiction books beginning with *Education: An American Problem* in 1968. But it was the tone Ayers had set in his latest book—*To Teach* (1993)—that Barack hoped to emulate."

Andersen makes a strong case for Ayers's active involvement in the crafting of *Dreams*. "To flesh out his family history, Barack had also taped interviews with Toot, Gramps, Ann, Maya, and his Kenyan relatives," Andersen writes. "These oral histories, along with his partial manuscript and a trunkload of notes, were given to Ayers."[125] Having been involved in many such projects myself, I find Andersen's description of the handoff of material entirely credible. Although Andersen did not consult with me on the book, he told me afterwards that he relied on two sources in Obama's Hyde Park neighborhood. Understandably, he would not reveal who those sources were.

Although Andersen's book was widely reviewed—he even appeared on *Hardball with Chris Matthews*—no one wanted to touch the six pages he spent on the writing of *Dreams*. This includes Garrow, who cites Andersen on several occasions in his Obama biography but ignores him on the question of authorship. My guess is that Garrow did not even read my 2011 book *Deconstructing Obama*, certainly not the section that follows:

Dreams tells us that Chicago's schools "remained in a state of perpetual crisis." "Navigating" describes the situation as a "perpetual state of conflict, paralysis, and stagnation."

Dreams describes a "bloated bureaucracy" as one source of the problem and "a teachers' union that went out on strike at least once every two years" as another. "Navigating" affirms that the "bureaucracy has grown steadily in the past decade" and confirms *Dreams'* math, citing a "ninth walkout in 18 years."

"Self-interest" is at the heart of the bureaucratic mess described in *Dreams*. "Navigating" clarifies that "survivalist bureaucracies" struggle for power "to protect their narrow, self-interested positions against any common, public purpose."

In *Dreams*, educators "defend the status quo" and blame problems on "impossible" children and their "bad parents." In "Navigating," an educator serves as "apologist for the status quo" and "place[s] the blame for school failure on children and families."

Another challenge cited in *Dreams* is "an indifferent state legislature." Ayers cites an "unwillingness on [the legislature's] part to adequately fund Chicago schools."

In *Dreams*, "school reform" is the only solution that Obama envisions. In "Navigating," Ayers has no greater passion than "reforming Chicago's schools."[126]

In fact, the year "Navigating" was published, 1994, was the same year Ayers coauthored the proposal that would win for Chicago a $49.2 million Annenberg Challenge grant and lead him to enlist Obama to chair it. My speculation is that chairing Annenberg was Obama's quid to the quo of Ayers's editorial help on *Dreams*.

In "Navigating" Ayers gives credence to those black activists who insisted that attacks on the largely black school bureaucracy were based "on simple Chicago race politics." Politically correct long before his time, he makes the case that, despite appearances, the white man was ultimately at fault for the current mess in Chicago schools. In *Dreams*, however, Obama takes the opposite tack. He observes, "The biggest source of resistance was rarely talked about," namely that black educators "would defend the status quo with the same skill and vigor as their white counterparts of two decades before."

If my thesis is correct, there is a wonderful irony at play here. Ayers has Obama lament that black obstinacy "was rarely talked about" without admitting that the people who should be talking about it were afraid to, none more so than the fellow who planted the thought in Obama's mind.

As to the claims of these black educators that "cutbacks in the bureaucracy were part of a white effort to wrest back control," Obama writes boldly, "not so true." This is a bold declaration. With these three words, we can begin to calculate Obama's potential return on Ayers's investment. Simply put, he could serve as the black front man for white operatives like Ayers. This is a role Obama would play time and again in his political career. In fact, my original title for *Unmasking Obama* was "Front Man."

Garrow also acknowledges, "Ayers had met Barack multiple times thanks to his lead role in staffing the Chicago School Reform Collaborative."[127] The date of these meetings is unspecified, but Garrow implies they took place after the first alleged meeting between Ayers and Obama in February 1995. The evidence in *Dreams* suggests, however, that these meetings took place well before the book was finished.

In *Dreams*, Obama openly criticizes the black educators who "knew too much" to send their own children to public school.[128] As it happens, the Obama of *Dreams* had a change of heart upon moving to Washington. As soon as he was elected president, he and Michelle made the same rational decision Chicago educators often made. After "a tour of D.C. schools," they decided to enroll Malia and Sasha in Sidwell

Friends—current tuition, forty-five thousand or so. If they considered public schools for their daughters, Obama does not mention it.

In *A Promised Land* Obama mentions neither the Chicago School Reform Collaborative nor the Annenberg Chicago Challenge, but he still talks a good game about public education. He tells us that he hoped to "place issues like inequality or lack of educational opportunity at the very center of the national debate and then actually deliver the goods." This meant "a topflight education for every child."[129] Every child, Obama meant, except the two thousand low-income students already afforded a topflight education in the District of Columbia.

In 2004, over Democratic opposition, President George W. Bush signed a law that resulted in the creation of what was called the DC Opportunity Scholarship Program (OSP). The highly successful and much-loved program—the first federal program anywhere to provide students with vouchers—enabled some two thousand DC children to attend private schools in the District.

When the Democrats took over Congress in 2007, they set out to eliminate the program. In June 2008, District congressional representative Eleanor Holmes Norton told the *Washington Post* with a logic the Queen of Hearts would admire, "We have to protect the children, who are the truly innocent victims here. But I can tell you that the Democratic Congress is not about to extend this program."[130]

Upon taking office in 2009, Obama held the fate of these two thousand lucky students in his hands. Obama boasts that his nearly trillion-dollar stimulus package "would finance one of the largest and most ambitious education reform agendas in a generation,"[131] but apparently there was not enough money for the DC Opportunity Scholarship Program. In March 2009, Obama's colleague from Illinois, Sen. Dick Durbin, slipped a poison pill into a pending four-hundred-billion-dollar omnibus spending bill. Durbin's provision would have prohibited any additional children from receiving scholarships unless the program was fully reauthorized by Congress and authorized by the DC City Council. Durbin would not have made this gesture without Obama's blessing.

People noticed; among them was syndicated black columnist and CNN contributor Roland Martin. "Some believe the Obama administration is sending mixed signals because Education Secretary Arne Duncan has said he doesn't want to see kids thrown out of Washington schools who are already in the existing voucher program," wrote Martin. "Fine. But the reality is that after this year, no new kids will be allowed to enroll in the program, and that folks, is killing the program."[132]

After Republican seized control of the House in the 2010 election, Speaker John Boehner secured the restoration and expansion of the program during what the *Daily Signal* called "heated budget negotiations."[133] In *A Promised Land* Obama speaks at length about other negotiating sessions, but he cannot spare a word for the OSP negotiation. In fact, the word "voucher" does not appear in the book. Nor is there any mention of the National Education Association (NEA), the teachers' union that sets Democratic education policy.

According to Obama, Boehner was as infected as the rest of the House majority by the same, super-spreading vibe that emanated from the Palin rallies—"an emotional, almost visceral, reaction to my presidency."[134] For no reason Obama bothers to explain, these crypto-racists were investing serious political capital in helping two thousand children, the great majority black, get a better education. Obama was not.

With Ayers repaid, Obama's debt going forward was to the NEA. In 2012, at its bidding, he was, as the *Daily Signal* phrased it, "once again standing with education special interest groups and against low-income children in Washington, D.C."[135] *A Promised Land* would have benefited greatly if Obama reflected on why he tried to shut down the DC OSP, but he is writing for an audience largely spared real-time news of this program's fight for life. His readers will not realize this story is missing from the book. And what a fascinating story it might have been. The first African American president stands in front of the Sidwell Friends schoolhouse door, staring down the thousands of black parents desperate to get their children in. Imagine the optics.

A Smaller and Smaller
Coil of Rage

Bill Ayers's input in *Dreams* was significant, too significant. Unlike a professional book doctor, he allowed his voice to cannibalize that of the named author—not everywhere, just in the more vital parts of the book. In Ayers's 2001 memoir, *Fugitive Days,* "rage" is the order of the day. Ayers tells of how his "rage got started" and how it morphed into an "uncontrollable rage—fierce frenzy of fire and lava." In October 1969, that rage exploded into the notorious "Days of Rage" in the streets of Chicago. Five years before Obama and his literary elves published *Audacity of Hope*, Ayers was writing, "I felt the warrior rising up inside of me—audacity and courage, righteousness, of course, and more audacity."

On the subject of *Dreams*, David Garrow and I agree on a few points. One is that a current of "rage" courses through *Dreams*. "The only thing you could choose as your own," writes Obama upon coming to terms with his blackness, "was withdrawal into a smaller and smaller coil of rage, until being black meant only the knowledge of your own powerlessness, of your own defeat."[136] So manifested is this theme that, as mentioned earlier, Dinesh D'Souza titled his bestseller, *The Roots of Obama's Rage.*

Garrow and I also agree that the sense of rage is largely manufactured. In describing the release of *Dreams* in 1995, Garrow reports reactions of "complete astonishment" from just about everyone who knew Obama. "The serene man his friends describe could not be more different from the person Obama himself describes in his memoir," one observer told Garrow. Many of Obama's acquaintances, black and white, told Garrow pretty much the same thing. "We had no clue," said one friend. "I never heard or felt or sensed any kind of identity crisis." [137]

Obama was not just reinventing his life in *Dreams*. He was crafting for himself a new persona. In fact, from Garrow's perspective, *Dreams* "was not a memoir or an autobiography; it was instead, in multitudinous ways, without any question a work of *historical fiction*." [138] Garrow understands as well the calculation behind the deception. Obama was positioning himself as an understandably angry black man to enhance his political appeal in black Chicago. As an ex-president Obama has shed this persona. In *A Promised Land*, he is back to being the "serene man" his friends have always known, at least when not reflecting on Trump, Palin, or the Tea Party. What Garrow refuses to consider is that someone provided Obama with the necessary rhetoric to express black rage.

We agree, however, that Obama did not write *Dreams* by himself. This would not be an issue were Obama humbler about his talents, but he hasn't been. On the campaign trail in 2008, he told a worshipful crowd of teachers. "I've written two books. I actually wrote them myself." [139] Here Obama was distinguishing himself from John McCain who gave his coauthor Mark Salter credit on the cover of their multiple books.

Obama, after all, had a reputation to live up to. On the strength of *Dreams*, British literary heavyweight Jonathan Raban declared Obama "the best writer to occupy the White House since Lincoln." Added Raban, "Every sentence has its own graceful cadence! He could as easily be a novelist as a politician!" [140] Raban was one among many literati who had put Obama on their virtual shoulders and paraded him around cyberspace as one of their own.

If I identify Ayers as Obama's muse, Garrow points to Obama's friend Rob Fisher, a white economist and law school buddy. "I was deeply involved with helping him sort of shape it," the "normally self-effacing" Fisher told Garrow. He also admitted to having "had a big influence" on the final product.[141] Seven years older than Obama and an established academic economist before starting law school, Fisher became good friends with Obama at Harvard. There, they coauthored a manuscript that, perhaps prophetically, was never finished. Obama had trouble finishing anything. He had to be prodded on multiple occasions to finish *Dreams* by both Michelle and his dutiful agent.

One completed chapter of Obama's book with Fisher dealt with the always-sexy topic of plant closings. "The quest is to develop guidelines," they wrote, "on how politically progressive movements can use the market mechanism to promote social goals." They were particularly keen on "worker ownership and control."

The second, more controversial chapter was titled "Race and Rights Rhetoric." Here, the authors describe America as "an admittedly racist culture" without acknowledging who has done the admitting. Garrow quotes the unfinished manuscript extensively. Its style is dependably wonkish and ungainly. There is no hint of "rage" about it. Sentences such as the following suggest that one author wrote as awkwardly as the other: "While Yuppies can afford the expensive frivolities provided by The Sharper Image, others receive insufficient nutrition to allow their minds to develop properly."[142]

This style evokes the Obama of 1983 whose published essay from that year, "Breaking the War Mentality," endorsed the KGB-driven anti-nuke crusade. More to the point, his writing style challenges all future claims of literary greatness. As an Ivy League senior, Obama would have been lucky to get a passing grade, let alone a Pulitzer, with such muddled sentences as, "What members of ARA and SAM try to do is infuse what they have learned about the current situation, bring the words of that formidable roster on the face of Butler Library, names like Thoreau, Jefferson, and Whitman, to bear on the twisted logic of which we are today a part."[143]

Strikingly, the only time Obama mentions *Dreams from My Father* by name in *A Promised Land* is when he evokes Trump's challenge to its legitimacy. He mentions at one point that he signed a contract "to write a book" and at another point that he "finished my book," and that was that. He makes no mention at all of Fisher. In reality, the process of

getting *Dreams* published was much messier and much more deserving
of an honest retelling.

As Christopher Andersen reports, in 1993 Simon & Schuster can-
celled its contract with Obama for a long overdue book and asked for a
return of the seventy-five thousand dollars already advanced. When he
pled poverty, the publisher did not press. Undaunted, his agent landed
Obama another deal, this one for forty thousand dollars with the Times
Book Division of Random House.

Needing a place to concentrate, the debt-ridden Obama headed not
to a basement office or to a nearby coffee shop, but to Bali, as in South
Pacific Bali, for six weeks without his new bride, Michelle. "With a
September 1994 deadline looming," writes Andersen, "Barack was still
stymied. It was around this time that, at Michelle's urging, he sought
advice from his friend and Hyde Park neighbor Bill Ayers."[144]

Garrow tells much the same story but attributes the book's restructur-
ing to Rob Fisher. He also adds considerable detail about Obama's work-
load both at his law firm and at the University of Chicago. According to
Garrow, Obama took six weeks off from his legal work in spring 1994
to finish the book. He was able to flesh out the Kenya portion thanks
to copies of letters he sent during a Kenya trip in 1988 provided by old
girlfriend Sheila Jager. "Michelle was ecstatic that the end of what was
now a four-year-long struggle was finally in sight," writes Garrow.[145]

David Maraniss adds still another wrinkle to this story. As Maraniss
relates in his biography, when Obama submitted the first draft of what
was now a memoir to Crown editor Henry Ferris, the draft did not
include the lengthy final section of the book, which dealt with Kenya.
This material, writes Maraniss, came from notes Obama made in his own
journal during a 1988 trip to Kenya. "I almost transcribed my journal
into the book," Obama told Maraniss.

Maraniss had previously interviewed Ferris. According to Ferris,
writes Maraniss, "Obama in fact traveled to Kenya a second time for
further research before turning in the last part of the book."[146] The language here is clear. Obama traveled to Africa after the first submission
of the book but before the final one. In his Oval Office interview with

Maraniss, Obama seems to have confirmed Ferris's account. "I did take a second trip to Africa, but all the stuff that I learned about the family, that was all in the first trip. The second trip was essentially me doing more background on things like Kenyan history. That was as close as I came to fact-checking, was that second trip. But that initial narrative, that I did not compress, that all happened on the first trip."[147]

As he often did, Maraniss left a potentially revealing story on the table. According to all accounts, Obama made only two trips to Africa before his election to the Senate in 2004: the first one in 1988 recounted in *Dreams* and the second one with Michelle in 1992. In Maraniss's report of the Oval Office interview, Obama makes no mention of Michelle accompanying him on the fact-checking trip or of the date of the trip. Besides, in 1992, Obama was still under contract with Simon & Schuster to write a book on race and voting rights.

There are a few possible explanations for the obvious holes in this account. An unlikely one is that Ferris incorrectly recalled Obama's return trip to Kenya, and Obama compounded this lapse by confirming it in his interview with Maraniss. A second possible explanation, intriguing but also unlikely, is that Obama did make a third trip to Kenya in 1994 and chose not to reveal it beyond his inner circle. In *A Promised Land*, Obama sheds no light on his trips to Kenya. When he mentions Kenya, it is usually to complain about people claiming he was born there.

A third possibility, and the most likely, is that Obama misled Ferris about making a return trip to Kenya, possibly to show how serious he was about finishing the book and getting his facts straight. Instead of going to Africa, Obama may have spent his six-week leave from his law firm pillaging the memoirs of longtime Kenya resident Kuki Gallmann. This is the thesis proposed by Shawn Glasco, a tireless researcher into all things Obama. Obama's evasions about his Kenya research trip make Glasco's theory all the more credible.

The Gallman book that most intrigued Glasco was *African Nights*, conveniently published in 1994. Glasco found scores of words and concepts that reappear all but intact in Obama's *Dreams*. Gallmann, for instance, tells the reader of a certain fellow. "He was a little man with a perennial grin" and a "readiness to obey or volunteer for any work." His "sentences often became tangled in a painful stutter." In *Dreams,* Obama meets "a short, gentle man with a bit of a stutter; he did odd jobs." On reading countless parallel sentences and phrases, the reader has to ask: Did Obama really know such a man, or has he borrowed from Gallman's experience?[148]

Similarly, in *Dreams,* Obama speaks of an improbable encounter with a young black boy alongside New York City's East River. The boy approaches this strange man and asks, "You know why sometimes the river runs that way and then sometimes it goes this way?" Obama tells the boy it "had to do with the tides." In his 1993 book, *To Teach,* Ayers tells the story of an adventurous teacher who would take her students out into the city to learn life lessons about the various sites, including the Hudson River. There, one student said, "Look, the river is flowing up." A second student said, "No, it has to flow south-down." The teacher revealed "that the Hudson River is a tidal river, that it flows both north and south, and they had visited the exact spot where the tide stops its northward push." I know, a coincidence.

Although Garrow is strongest on detail, he blinded himself to the obvious involvement of Ayers, of whom Khalidi writes in the acknowledgment section of his 2004 book, *Resurrecting Empire,* "First, chronologically and in other ways comes Bill Ayers."[149] As an aspiring politico, Obama could not to afford give Ayers the public strokes their mutual friend Khalidi did.

I don't doubt that Rob Fisher was involved, but he did not lend the book its fire. Ayers did. Ayers did not "write" *Dreams.* He doctored it, indifferent to the fact that he was helping reshape Obama's persona. Obama could have used his touch on *A Promised Land.* The Obama of *Dreams* was considerably less real but much more interesting.

Subprime Lending Started Off as a Good Idea

"You never want a serious crisis to go to waste," said Rahm Emanuel in November 2008 as the nation was slogging through the detritus of the subprime meltdown.[150] Two months later, Emanuel would take his place as President Obama's chief of staff. With an able assist from the media, Obama had ridden the crisis all the way to the White House.

A Promised Land is written for those who either don't know what caused the financial meltdown of 2008 or those who don't care to be reminded. Typical is *New York Times* book reviewer, Jennifer Szalai. So matter-of-factly does she blame the crisis on Republican "deregulatory policies" that it is clear she expects no pushback.[151] In reading the reviews, I am reminded just how deeply propagandized liberals have been by their own media. For those who do know about the causes of the subprime crisis, and especially those who know Obama's tangential but telling role in causing it, *A Promised Land* is a painful read, an extended exercise in mendacity.

In his memoir, Obama tells of how in September 2007 he delivered a speech at Nasdaq "decrying the failure to regulate the subprime lending market and proposing stronger oversight."[152] In fact, Obama did give a speech at Nasdaq on September 17, 2007, and he did mention the subprime crisis, albeit halfway into the speech after lots of boilerplate about FDR and the need for honesty and transparency on Wall Street.

Not knowing how far south things were about to go at the time, Obama told his Wall Street audience, "Subprime lending started off as a good idea—helping Americans buy homes who couldn't previously afford to."[153] He then quickly shifted to a lecture on how "the unscrupulous practice of some bad actors" turned this good idea bad.

In *A Promised Land*, Obama deep-sixes the "good idea" memory and disavows all responsibility for what happened in 2008. From his comfortable perch in Martha's Vineyard twelve years later, he writes of government in general and himself in particular as the saviors of Wall Street, not its seducers.

Obama's discussion of the crisis and the ensuing bailout is lengthy and, by his standards, relatively nuanced. He concedes that "plenty of congressional Democrats had applauded rising homeownership rates throughout the subprime boom" and offers students of history some useful insider nuggets. What historians will not find, however, is even a hint that Obama's allies deserve the jackal's share of responsibility for the subprime mess. As reflective as Obama appears, at least to his fans, he consciously fails to assess his and his party's role in creating the crisis they exploited.

Many readers of Obama's memoir, I suspect, have little understanding of what a subprime loan is and why lenders would make one. Obama would just as soon keep it that way. To explain would be to reveal the fact that these loans were never a "good idea." Like most politicians, Obama uses "subprime" as an adjective to describe a kind of loan when it would be more accurately used to describe a kind of borrower. The word "loan" helps shift the moral burden to the lender.

In the way of background, engineer Bill Fair and mathematician Earl Isaac started the Fair Isaac Corporation in 1956. To measure credit risk, they devised a model, now called FICO, which gauges a would-be borrower's ability to handle credit based on how he or she handled it in the past. Lenders consider a borrower with a FICO score in the 650 to

850 range a "prime" credit prospect. Those who score beneath 650 are considered "subprime."

Lenders have historically solicited prime prospects. Given their lack of legitimate options, subprime borrowers typically have had to pay more interest to secure a loan. These borrowers have kept pawnbrokers and loan sharks in business for millennia and, more recently, have made the payday loan industry a going concern.

One of Obama's Chicago mentors, civil rights activist John McKnight, had a problem with the traditional business model as it played out in real life. Believing that lenders discriminated against black borrowers for the simple reason they were black, he helped lay the intellectual groundwork for the passage of the Community Reinvestment Act. McKnight, in fact, was known as "the father of the CRA."[154]

Passed in 1977 during the Jimmy Carter presidency, the CRA merely "encouraged" lenders to "help meet the credit needs of local communities." Under President Bill Clinton, regulators moved from encouraging to strong-arming. McKnight was on the front line of the battles to come. Like many in Obama's orbit, McKnight has argued that housing is a right and that lenders should serve citizens much the way public utilities do.

An acolyte of the crypto-Marxist Saul Alinsky, McKnight claims to have given Obama his first community organizing assignment in Chicago. "I was one of those involved in his training," McKnight writes of Obama. "He was a thoughtful, wise and balanced young man. What he learned was a kind of neighborhood organizing that was developed by Saul Alinsky. The method is described in Alinsky's classic book, *Reveille for Radicals*."[155]

"He was a Alinsky organizer," confirmed another white Chicago mentor, Gerald Kellman. "The Alinsky organizer talks about self-interest," he told a PBS interviewer in 2008. "And what you would learn from that is that: Don't pretend the world as it is is the world as you would like it to be. Get realistic."[156]

A friendly 2008 article in the *New York Times* casually acknowledged the connection. "The small organization Mr. Obama worked for, the Developing Communities Project, was influenced by the thinking of

Saul Alinsky," wrote the *Times'* Serge Kovaleski. "Mr. Alinsky viewed self-interest as the main motivation for political participation."[157]

In 1990, Obama contributed an essay titled, "Why Organize?" to a collection called *After Alinsky: Community Organizing in Illinois.* Although Obama shied from the gonzo tactics Alinsky used to get press attention, he embraced the use of Alinsky-driven power strategies to mobilize the collective will of the community. In his article, he also favorably cited McKnight's influence. "The problems facing inner-city communities do not result from a lack of effective solutions," wrote Obama, "but from a lack of power to implement these solutions."[158]

Despite the abundant evidence, Obama bristles at those on the right who criticized "my alleged fealty to radical community organizer Saul Alinsky." In *A Promised Land*, he equates that charge to accusations about "my friendship with my neighbor Bill Ayers."[159] In reality, his connection to Alinsky no more deserves the word "alleged" than does his friendship with "neighbor" Bill Ayers.

Kill Him!

As the subprime cancer metastasized, Obama had no excuse for not seeing the symptoms. Upon returning from law school, and after taking a year off his career track to run Project Vote, Obama joined Davis, Miner, Barnhill & Galland. This law firm, he tells us, "did real estate work for affordable housing groups."

Meanwhile Obama mentor John McKnight was using the National People's Action (NPA), a group he cofounded, to coerce lenders into giving loans to poor people. While Clinton's regulators were pressuring regulators where they worked, busloads of goons from the NPA were attacking bankers where they lived. Shouting, "Housing is a right, and we're going to take it," they trashed the bankers' yards and frightened their families.

The notorious ACORN, shorthand for Association of Community Organizations for Reform Now, used many of the same tactics. In 1991, back before occupying the Capitol was seen as a bad thing, its activists took over the House Banking Committee hearing room. They hoped to embarrass bankers into making loans to people they had historically turned down. "If there was no community pressure and the law, few banks would do something," ACORN's housing director Michael Shea told the *New York Times*.[160]

An increasing left-leading media romanticized ACORN and, in doing so, amplified its power. "The nation's largest banks have come to the negotiating table just to silence objections that could derail or create costly delays to a merger," the *Times* reported. The article quoted a federal regulator who gave his blessing to ACORN's extortion: "Acorn is street-tough and they bedevil the bankers. But they've gotten banks to commit millions they otherwise would not have lent."[161] ACORN's enforcers harassed lenders and blocked their plans to expand into new markets unless they could show they were "CRA-compliant." ACORN also lobbied a "reluctant" Fannie Mae to buy the loans that ACORN activists had pressured the banks into making.

In 2008, ACORN's corruption was too blatant for even the *New York Times* to ignore. Wrote the *Times* a month before the election, "It made news this year when it was revealed that a brother of Acorn's founder had embezzled almost $1 million from the organization but that Acorn had failed to disclose the theft for eight years."[162] Although *Times* reporter Stephanie Strom did her best to minimize Obama's ties to ACORN, she had to concede that the claims of the McCain camp were largely true.

Yes, Obama did represent ACORN in a 1995 voter access lawsuit. Yes, the Obama camp did pay an ACORN affiliate nearly a million dollars for a get-out-the-vote effort despite ACORN's reputation for voter fraud. Yes, the Obama camp did falsely report that the payment was for "staging, sound, lighting" and other advance work. Yes, Obama did say to ACORN officials, "When I ran Project Vote voter registration drives in Illinois, Acorn was smack dab in the middle of it, and we appreciate your work." Yes, ACORN's political action committee did endorse Obama for president. And yes, Obama had done training for the group. "What were you teaching them?" McCain adviser Rick Davis suggested the media ask Obama. "Were you teaching them how to evade the law?"

For its part, ACORN claimed that investigations into its voter registration work were "politically motivated." Besides, as ACORN honcho Bertha Lewis assured Strom, "Rumors of Acorn's voter fraud have been greatly exaggerated and to a large extent manufactured," a roundabout way of saying, "We haven't stolen quite as many votes as we are accused of."

One Strom article might have affected the outcome of the election, but it perished on the editor's desk. Strom had been speaking with former ACORN employee Anita MonCrief. MonCrief would testify in a Pennsylvania court that during the 2008 campaign the Obama people gave ACORN a list of contributors who had already given the legal limit to Obama. The understanding was that ACORN would use whatever money it raised from these donors to help the Obama campaign. Fortunately for Obama, the *Times* never ran the story. MonCrief recorded Strom telling her, "I have just been asked by my bosses to stand down. They want me to hold off on coming to Washington. Sorry, I take my orders from higher up sometimes."

Despite all this drama, Obama makes no mention of McKnight, Kellman, National People's Action, or the stunningly corrupt ACORN in *A Promised Land*. This silence is all the more notable given that Sarah Palin was the one who repeatedly tied ACORN around Obama's neck. "In this election, it's a choice between a candidate who won't disavow a group committing voter fraud, and a leader who won't tolerate voter fraud," Palin told her audiences.[163]

Obama apparently did not want to go there. "From the stage, she accused me of 'palling around with terrorists who would target their own country,'" whines Obama about Palin. "She suggested that I was 'not a man who sees America the way you and I see America.' People turned up at rallies wearing T-shirts bearing slogans like PALIN'S PITBULLS and NO COMMUNISTS."[164] This is all true, but why no mention of Palin's attacks on ACORN, especially given that ACORN and its media allies routinely countercharged its accusers with racism, a tactic with which Obama was, and is, much too comfortable?

Did I mention Obama was obsessed with Palin? He repeats the accusation that someone at a Palin rally once yelled, "Kill him!" The "kill him" charge received an absurd amount of attention considering its dubious provenance. The media never identified the man accused and, scarier still, never came to agreement as to where he launched his verbal assault. The lack of evidence should have killed the story in the womb or at least raised the possibility of an *agent provocateur*. It did neither. The story lives on in Obama's imagination and, now, that of his readers.

Ahab was less obsessed with his whale—also white—than Obama is with Palin. "Through Palin," grouses Obama, "it seemed as if the dark spirits that had long been lurking on the edges of the modern Republican Party—xenophobia, anti-intellectualism, paranoid conspiracy theories, an antipathy toward Black and brown folks—were finding their way to center stage." If I might digress, among Obama's more annoying stylistic tics is his use of the word "folks" to designate people of color. Among his more profound failures as a president and as a person is his refusal to understand ordinary people who are not of color, from Joe the Plumber to Sarah Palin to Toot, the grandmother who raised him.

Knee-Deep in the Subprime Market

O f all the stories Obama omits from *A Promised Land*, certainly in regard to the subprime crisis, one stands out. In 1994, while working as an attorney with Davis Miner, Obama helped his firm bring a class action suit against Citibank. Obama's clients were Chicago area African Americans who claimed they had been rejected for home loans simply because they were black. In taking the case, Obama refused to acknowledge why blacks fall behind whites and Asians and even Hispanics on a wide range of social variables, home ownership among them.

When Bill Clinton was inaugurated in 1993, the national home ownership rate was *lower* across the board than it had been when Richard Nixon was inaugurated in 1969. As Obama should have known, the growth in single-parent families, especially in the black community, was negating the increase in general prosperity. How could it not? In 1993, the average income for households headed by divorced women was 40 percent that of married couples; for unmarried women it was only 20 percent. This had nothing to do with race but everything to do with family. As the numbers suggest, many of these women could not manage homes of their own. Home-ownership rates for female-headed households struggled to stay above 50 percent.

For married couples, home-ownership rates hovered consistently in the 80-percentile range. With blacks overrepresented among single families—by 1993, 57 percent of black children were growing up in a single-parent household as compared to 21 percent of white children—black home-ownership rates were lower than those for whites or Asians. In the early 1990s that gap was at least twenty-five percentage points, around 70 percent for whites and in the low 40s for blacks.[165]

In suing Citibank, Obama refused to acknowledge the role family breakdown played in the lending industry. Yes, a 1991 study by the Federal Reserve found that 61 percent of blacks had been approved in their quest for government-backed home loans as compared to 77 percent for whites, but even that study conceded a lack of information about "the creditworthiness of applicants" as well as "the adequacy of the collateral offered."[166]

For "civil rights" activists like Obama and his media allies these limitations were mere quibble. They *wanted* to believe—and wanted America to believe—that lenders in late-century America would willingly sacrifice their own profits to keep the black man down, and they were not about to let facts stand in the way.

To make the racism story line work, Obama and his colleagues had to overlook default rates. In 2004, HUD did a study of FHA loans that originated in 1992. The sample size was large, nearly two hundred fifty thousand loans, and the cross-racial data were for comparable properties. The study revealed that after seven largely prosperous years from 1992 to 1999, blacks were defaulting on their home loans more than twice as frequently as whites. Were blacks held to tougher standards, as Obama's Citibank suit insisted, black default rates should have been lower than whites, not higher.[167]

Obama had to know about the effect of family dynamics on home ownership. Indifferent to the data, he and his partners charged Citibank with denying their plaintiffs first mortgage loans "on the basis of their race or the racial composition of their neighborhoods." For its part, Citibank rejected "each and every claim of wrongdoing."[168] Still, the company agreed to settle as Obama's partners knew it would. When media observers are all pulling for David, no one wants to play the role Goliath, especially a Goliath wearing a white hood. Not surprisingly, Obama's law firm pocketed in fees nearly three times what the aggrieved parties received in payment. As part of the settlement, Citibank agreed to organize a lending consortium in Chicago to "assist low to moderate income loan applicants in obtaining mortgages." If Obama did not cause the subprime crisis, it was not for want of trying.

ACORN had been softening the ground for the plaintiffs by staging a series of protests and meeting at the Citibank headquarters in Manhattan. In fact, the Chicago suit was one of eleven launched against Citibank. The result of the shakedown, wrote ACORN head Wade Rathke in 2004, was that "thousands of lower income families might actually become homeowners in our neighborhoods." Rathke also claimed to believe that for Citibank, "it could mean acquiring significant share of this market and making millions in profits from a customer base that they now wanted, but had not traditionally had."[169] No, until coerced, Citibank execs wanted no share of this market, but, like many of their peers, they were prepared to make lemonade out of subprime lemons.

With a gun to their head, the lenders turned to Fannie Mae and Freddie Mac to relieve them of the imprudent loans they were now being forced to make. Before the 1990s, Fannie and Freddie had sufficiently tough lending standards that default was not much of an issue. That would change. In 1999, the newly appointed CEO, Franklin Delano Raines, was boasting of the reforms Fannie Mae had already made and the reforms to come. As he told the *Times*, Fannie Mae had lowered the down payment requirements for a home and now planned to extend credit to borrowers a "notch below" its traditional standards.[170] That notch was spelled *subprime*.

The Wall Street end of the "notch below" story is well enough known to those who care to know. That does not include most Democrats. Kept in the dark by the media, they still labor under the illusion that Wall Street was a Republican thing. By 2008, however, Democrats had a grip on Wall Street almost as firm as their grip on Hollywood or the media. As the *Los Angeles Times* reported in March 2008, "Hillary Rodham Clinton and Barack Obama, who are running for president as economic populists, are benefiting handsomely from Wall Street donations, easily surpassing Republican John McCain in campaign contributions from the troubled financial services sector."[171] Despite his extensive discussion of Wall Street in *A Promised Land*, Obama does not share this revealing intel.

For investors, high interest translated into high yield. In October 1997, the investment banks Bear Stearns and First Union Capital Markets underwrote the first securitization of subprime loans for a total of $385 million. The triple-A rating of Freddie Mac–approved loans seemed, at least, to guarantee the payments on these securities. The virtue-signaling press release announcing the launch hit all the PC hot buttons: these "affordable" and "flexible" mortgages offered the possibility of credit for "low and moderate income families" in "traditionally underserved markets."[172]

These securities offered a 7.5 percent yield in a low-interest environment and, even better, a chance to purge one's predatory soul through an act of seeming charity. Imagining himself as a hedge fund manager who had been drinking too much progressive Kool-Aid, satirist Michael Lewis wrote, "At the time I bought the subprime portfolio, I thought: This is sort of like my way of giving something back."[173]

In his farewell address at the Democratic National Convention in August 2000, the recently impeached president—back when you had to be president to be impeached—boasted of "the highest home ownership rate in our history." At the time, the figure had moved beyond 67 percent and was still rising. Never shy about his accomplishments, real or imagined, President Clinton thanked the gathered Democrats for supporting his agenda, one that "has taken our country to new heights of prosperity, progress, and peace."[174]

In *A Promised Land*, Obama concedes that Fannie Mae and Freddie Mac were "knee deep in the subprime market" but chooses not to tell us how they got that way. Politics had more than a little to do with it. To rally the Democratic base a week before the 2000 election, Clinton squeezed Fannie and Freddie a little harder, upping their "affordable housing" quota from 42 to 50 percent. "These new regulations will greatly enhance access to affordable housing for minorities, urban residents, new immigrants and others left behind, giving millions of families the opportunity to buy homes," said clueless HUD Secretary Andrew Cuomo. "We acknowledge and appreciate that Fannie Mae and Freddie Mac have accepted this challenge."[175]

The hacks running these "private" enterprises did not protest the new quotas, certainly not publicly. "We have not been a major presence in the subprime market," said Fannie CEO Raines, "but you can bet that under these goals, we will be." Fannie's CFO, Timothy Howard, added, "making loans to people with less-than-perfect credit" is "something we should do."[176] As Raines and pals would soon learn, and quickly forget, the road to hell is paved with good ideas.

Almost Forty and Broke

The Bush administration deserves a share of the credit for the economic meltdown but not for any imagined deregulation. In 2003, at President Bush's urging, Congress passed the American Dream Downpayment Assistance Act. Said Federal Housing Commissioner John Weicher, "The White House doesn't think those who can afford the monthly payment but have been unable to save for a down payment should be deprived from owning a home."[177] Sarah Palin thought otherwise.

"Let's do what our parents told us before we probably even got that first credit card," Palin said in her debate with Biden. "Don't live outside of our means. We need to make sure that as individuals we're taking personal responsibility through all of this."[178]

On the issue of personal responsibility, Obama had cause to wonder whether Palin's barb was directed his way. He and Michelle lived chronically outside their means. In his memoir, Obama tells a revealing story about his trip to Los Angeles in the year 2000 to attend the Democratic convention. When Obama arrived at LAX and tried to rent a car, he was turned down because his "American Express card was over its limit." The credentials a friend had promised him, he discovered, did not allow him access to the convention floor. "Almost forty" and "broke," Obama ended up spending the night on his friend's couch and heading back to Chicago just as Al Gore gave his acceptance speech. "In other words,"

Obama concludes this cautionary tale, "I had become the very thing that, as a younger man, I had warned myself against. I had become a politician—and not a very good one at that."[179]

Nor obviously was he a very good manager of money. Although Michelle got her Harvard Law degree in 1988 and Obama his three years later, Barack and Michelle were notoriously swamped by debt. It took the booming sales of *Dreams* after the 2004 convention to bail them out. Although both were well employed—Michelle claims to have made more than one hundred thousand dollars a year right out of law school[180]—their history as a couple is a history of living beyond their means. Christopher Andersen speaks of them successively as "deeply in debt," "drowning in debt," and "still deeply in debt." Yet, despite the debt, the couple traveled to Kenya in 1992, and Obama sojourned to Bali a year later. Before the Kenya trip, Michelle "had been to Jamaica and the Bahamas, and to Europe a few times."[181] Andersen concludes, "They have grappled with financial problems, remaining deeply in debt well into their forties."[182]

It is no wonder Obama took offense at Rick Santelli's famed 2009 "rant" on CNBC about personal responsibility. He quotes Santelli as saying, "The government is promoting bad behavior! How many of you people want to pay for your neighbor's mortgage that has an extra bathroom and can't pay their bills?" In one of his very few uses of foul language, Obama drops a "bullshit" on Santelli's "half-baked populism." The fact that Santelli's "shtick" launched the Tea Party movement irks Obama all the more.[183]

The problem for America, as Santelli implied, was that political people no more fiscally responsible than Obama were tasked with managing the fiscal policies of the world. Among the more irresponsible was Fannie Mae's CEO Franklin Raines. Although the *New York Times* was sounding warning bells about Fannie Mae as early as August 2003, Raines deflected criticism by focusing on Fannie Mae's success at social engineering. "We have met or exceeded our affordable housing goals, even as they have increased," he told the House Committee on Financial

Services in late 2003. He also shared the company's "voluntary goal," namely, to "lead the market in serving minority families."[184]

Raines had equally irresponsible friends in Congress. At that same hearing, Congresswoman Maxine Waters commended "the outstanding leadership of Frank Raines" and insisted that regulatory reform not impede Fannie Mae's "affordable housing mission, a mission that has seen innovation flourish from desktop underwriting to 100 percent loans."[185] Another friend was bubble-boy-in-chief Barney Frank, the ranking Democrat on House Committee on Financial Services. In 2005, on the House floor, he scolded his more prudent colleagues, "You are not going to see the collapse that you see when people talk about a bubble. So those on our committee in particular are going to continue to push for homeownership."[186]

In *A Promised Land*, Obama has only good things to say about Frank, "the tough and quick-witted Democrat from Massachusetts who knew his stuff."[187] About Franklin Raines, he has nothing to say. In July 2008, the *Washington Post*'s Anita Huslin caused Obama a minor headache by linking Raines, an African American and a Harvard Law grad, to the Obama campaign. Four years after leaving Fannie Mae under the cloud of a $6.3 billion accounting scandal, Raines had "shaved eight points off his golf handicap, taken a corner office in Steve Case's D.C. conglomeration of finance, entertainment and health-care companies and more recently, taken calls from Barack Obama's presidential campaign seeking his advice on mortgage and housing policy matters." The McCain campaign noticed the *Post* article and began running ads based on Huslin's reporting.

The Obama campaign, of course, denied any connection to Raines. Although conceding the subprime woes of the "quasi-governmental" Fannie Mae and Freddie Mac, he exonerates the federal government from any responsibility for the performance of these "two giant companies." Obama writes, "Congress had authorized [them] to purchase qualified mortgages to encourage homeownership."[188] The fact that the Clinton administration, its appointees at Fannie Mae and Freddie Mac, Obama's friends at ACORN and the NPA, and Obama's own law firm were defining "qualified" down does not factor into Obama's reflections.

In *A Promised Land,* Obama writes that he first took notice of the impending crisis in the spring of 2007 when New Century Financial declared bankruptcy and Countrywide Financial Corporation almost did. In 1994, Countrywide had, in fact, been the first major lender to sign a "voluntary" deal with HUD to make more loans to high-risk borrowers. At the time, HUD was investigating Countrywide for discrimination. CEO Angelo Mozilo had little choice but to play along. He launched a comprehensive cultural diversity program and doubled Countrywide's minority loans. The Clinton administration had hired hundreds of new bank examiners to identify "racist" practices. Lenders like Mozilo did what they had to do to stay on Washington's good side.[189]

Things went swimmingly for Mozilo and his peers until they didn't. Rising interest rates squeezed his high-risk borrowers. When they began to default, real estate prices started to decline. More and more homeowners found themselves underwater as did the virtuous investment banks that made homeownership possible for just about anyone willing to put a signature on an unread document.

In June 2008, the media reported on the details of a racket known informally as Friends of Angelo, or FOA. FOA waived points, lender fees, and borrowing rules for politically useful allies, among them Franklin Raines and chairman of the Senate Banking Committee, Christopher Dodd.[190] Angelo's friends could help only so much. On July 1, 2008, the Bank of America put the faltering giant out of its misery and bought it for $4.25 a share, one-tenth of its share price just eighteen months earlier.

Connecticut Senator Dodd had another friend in Joe Cassano of AIG, the Connecticut-based insurance company that underwrote many of the investment banks' subprime securities. Cassano had donated heavily to Dodd's senate campaigns as well as to his ill-conceived run for president in 2008 and had personally solicited contributions for Dodd from his employees.[191] Hedging his bets, Cassano contributed to Obama's primary run and maxed out in the general election for Obama. By this time, though, Cassano was investing only to save his skin. AIG was on the brink.

Fortunately for Cassano, his campaign investment paid off. The same failed politician who had his credit card bounce at the 2000 Democratic convention was accepting his party's nomination at the 2008 one. After the obligatory patter about "the young man from Kenya and a young woman from Kansas," Obama got to the meat of the matter. "More of you have cars you can't afford to drive, credit card bills you can't afford to pay, and tuition that's beyond your reach," preached Obama. "These challenges are not all of government's making. But the failure to respond is a direct result of a broken politics in Washington and the failed policies of George W. Bush."[192] For Obama, it was that simple.

As the subprime market cratered, the major Wall Street firms, led by Goldman Sachs, demanded that AIG honor its insurance policies. AIG did not have the capital to cover its clients' bad bets. Goldman Sachs, however, did not despair. The firm had friends in high places: Henry "Hank" Paulson was secretary of the treasury under Bush; former Goldman Sachs honcho, Robert Rubin, held the same job under Clinton; and ex-chief Jon Corzine was governor of New Jersey. Paulson persuaded the leaders of both parties to cover AIG's losses at the swaps table, $182 billion and counting, and pay its creditors one hundred cents on the dollar. If Wall Street breathed a little easier, Sarah Palin found it "very disappointing" that taxpayers were called on "to bail out another one."[193]

In *A Promised Land*, Obama recounts at great length how he, though still a candidate, and Paulson masterfully managed to get the Troubled Asset Relief Program (TARP) passed. "But while TARP's passage would prove to be critical in saving the financial system," Obama writes, "the whole episode did nothing to reverse the public's growing impression that the GOP—and by extension their nominee for president—couldn't be trusted to responsibly handle the crisis."[194] So said the man who just a few years earlier couldn't responsibly handle his own credit cards.

Obama wonders why the Wall Street executives, "whose collective asses we were pulling out of the fire,"[195] were not more grateful. To those who choose to know, the answer is pretty simple. The *we*—Carter,

Clinton, Obama, Dodd, Frank, Cuomo, Raines—lured the execs into the fire, even shoved them in when it suited their purposes. The execs knew this even if the Democratic faithful preferred to remain ignorant.

In *A Promised Land*, Obama acknowledges the anonymous forces on the left who questioned his timidity. They wondered why he did not seize the "once-in-a-generation chance to reset the standards for normalcy, re-making not just the financial system but the American economy overall," or, at the very least, send "some white-collar culprits to jail."[196] Obama claims to share their frustrations and questions whether he should have been "bolder." Had he been bolder, however, and put Wall Street on trial, Wall Street would have had no recourse but to tell the truth about the cause of the "Great Recession." Had that happened, Democrats would have not seen headlines like this one in a July 2011 *Washington Post*: "Obama campaign attracts Wall Street money, despite tensions."[197] In Washington, as on Wall Street, silence is golden.

There's No Such Thing as Shovel-Ready Projects

L ess than a month after Obama took office in 2009, he signed into law a 1,073-page bill that went by the name "the American Recovery and Reinvestment Act." For simplicity's sake, I will refer to it as the "Stimulus." Rush Limbaugh referred to it as "Porkulus," and he was altogether on target.

As he does throughout *A Promised Land*, Obama focuses more on the passage of the bill than he does on its consequences. Laboring under the illusion that the Stimulus was undeniably good for America, he traces opposition to the bill to the growing extremism among congressional Republicans. At the root of their resistance, of course, is an implicit racism nurtured by "a steady diet of Fox News, talk radio, and Sarah Palin speeches."[198]

Sarah Palin was problem enough, but in the fight to pass the Stimulus with bipartisan support Obama faced an even more formidable foe, the "billionaire ideologues" David and Charles Koch. In his memoir, Obama accuses the Kochs of doing what his own ally George Soros had actually been doing, namely spending "hundreds of millions of dollars systematically building a network of think tanks, advocacy organizations, media operations, and political operatives." Soros goes unmentioned in *A Promised Land*. During the Trump presidency, Obama watched

88

approvingly as any number of other billionaire ideologues—Jack Dorsey, Mark Zuckerberg, Jeff Bezos, Tom Steyer, Michael Bloomberg—threw their hundreds of millions into the fray. Collectively, Obama's billionaire allies had magnitudes more clout than the Kochs, who, as it happened, also opposed Trump.

The Kochs' opposition to Trump buys them no grace from Obama, who insists on punishing them anew even though David, the more politically active brother, died more than a year before his book's release. Obama needlessly cheapens his memoir by allowing hyperbole to stand for fact in his postmortem on the Kochs. From his perspective, the brothers had the "express goal of rolling back every last vestige of the modern welfare state." He writes, "They didn't want compromise and consensus. They wanted war."[199]

Libertarians to the core, the Kochs really just wanted to be left alone. In the lead-up to the 2010 midterms, it was Obama and his people who waged war on the Kochs, demonizing them to the point that the brothers had to hire security details for themselves and their families. It got so bad, in fact, that David felt obliged to send his children to school in a bulletproof car. "I'm not sure it would ever cross Charles's mind," a Koch friend observed, "that a sitting president would single him out."[200]

As he does throughout the book, Obama writes for an audience that sustained itself on the media's myopic, mean-spirited narratives for the eight years of his presidency. One of the canards that he pushes in the book is that the Kochs were the puppeteers behind the hated Tea Party. From experience, I can vouch that there was no puppeteer. I attended the initial Tea Party rally in Kansas City on April 15, 2009. I knew the organizer. A nineteen-year-old coed, she expected about two hundred people to show up. More than four thousand did. This was the norm across America. The passion was real. The Republicans in Congress respected that passion, as did the Kochs. Although both tried to exploit that passion, they could not begin to control it.

The identity-obsessed Obama offers a first take upon meeting the House Republicans that is as petty as it is predictable: "It was hard not to be struck by the room's uniformity: row after row of mostly middle-aged white men, with a dozen or so women and maybe two or three Hispanics and Asians."[201] The questions they posed to Obama upon first meeting were solid. One asked about the "Democratic-sponsored laws" that triggered the financial crisis. Another asked whether the Stimulus would repeat the mistakes of the New Deal in prolonging the financial crisis. A third asked, reasonably enough, "Mr. President, will you get Nancy Pelosi to put her partisan bill aside and start over with the truly open process that the American people are demanding?"[202]

This is the only occasion in the book that readers hear anything about Democrats causing the financial crisis. This is likely the first time in their lives most have heard that the New Deal prolonged the financial woes of Depression America. Obama includes the first two seemingly absurd questions to make the third seem absurd as well. It wasn't. One week after Obama's inauguration, the Republicans were presented with a thousand-page bill that came with a nearly trillion-dollar price tag. What possible reason could they have for being wary of it?

Writing ten years after the Stimulus was passed, Obama counts on his audience to forget the magic incantation he used to rally Democrats to the cause. In *A Promised Land*, he chooses not to remind them. On a December 2008 *Meet the Press* Obama shared the Stimulus mantra with the American public. "I think we can get a lot of work done fast," he told Tom Brokaw. "When I met with the governors, all of them have projects that are shovel ready, that are going to require us to get the money out the door, but they've already lined up the projects, and they can make them work."[203]

Yes, *shovel-ready*, a phrase that does not appear in the memoir. Obama and his people would repeat that promise as often and as earnestly as they would later swear, "If you like your doctor, you can keep your doctor." A week after Obama signed the Stimulus into law, he explained to Congress what "shovel ready" would look like when implemented. Using another magical phrase, "save or create," he promised three-and-half-million jobs that would not exist without the Stimulus, 90 percent of them in the private sector. The examples Obama cited were all brawny, broad-shouldered, New Deal kind of jobs—"rebuilding our roads and bridges; constructing wind turbines and solar panels; laying broadband and expanding mass transit."[204]

The value of this promise depreciated so quickly and visibly that Obama felt compelled to own up to it. Eight months after the bill was passed, an abashed president told a roomful of local government officials and union reps, "The term 'shovel-ready'—let's be honest, it doesn't always live up to its billing." By this time, less than 1 percent of the stimulus funds had been paid out. To paper over the difference between promise and performance Obama used a host of what the normally sympathetic FactCheck.org called "weasel words."[205] By October 2010, Obama was admitting to the *New York Times*, "There's no such thing as shovel-ready projects."[206]

One other promise Obama made to Brokaw in December 2008 proved equally as vaporous. "You know, the days of just pork coming out of Congress as a strategy," he told Brokaw, "those days are over."[207] Well, no, they weren't over. In fact, the Stimulus years were to pork what the sixties were to drugs or the seventies were to disco. True, some actual digging went into the three-million-dollar tunnel that allowed turtles safe passage under a Florida highway, but it is hard to imagine how shovels might have been employed to study erectile dysfunction in San Francisco–area fat men or to research the evolution of waterfowl genitalia. The word "pork" nicely defines these and scores of other equally spurious projects.[208]

Were there a competition for the most dishonest chapter in *A Promised Land*, the Stimulus chapter would certainly be a contender. Shoveling most vestiges of reality down the memory hole, Obama congratulates himself for passing this "historic legislation." Although he managed to secure the support of only three Republicans, each of whom, Obama concedes, had to be bought off, he compares the Recovery Act to the New Deal. "Any one of these items, if passed as a stand-alone bill, would qualify as a major achievement for a presidential administration," Obama concludes. "Taken together, they might represent the successful work of an entire first term."[209]

Readers of *A Promised Land* will have no idea how objectively ineffectual the Stimulus proved to be. Mitt Romney did, which is why he "demolished" Obama in their first debate in 2012. "When the president took office, 32 million people on food stamps; 47 million on food stamps today," said Romney. "Economic growth this year slower than last year, and last year slower than the year before. Going forward with the status quo is not going to cut it for the American people who are struggling today."[210] Obama had no answer.

Warts and Unwanted Compromises

By April 2009, bubble boy Barney Frank was denying that he had ever advocated homeownership for subprime borrowers. Without blushing, he told PBS's Tavis Smiley that he had long been an advocate for decent rental housing. "When people are making, frankly, $30,000 or $40,000 a year in much of this country, they're not going to be able to afford a home. And if you pretend that they can, you get them into trouble."[211] The subprime "trouble" he attributed to the "conservative view that rental housing was a bad thing." Meanwhile Friend of Angelo Christopher Dodd was giving new life to the phrase "damned if you, damned if you don't." Instead of back pats, he was now denouncing lenders as "unconscionable" for having made loans to "lower-income and unsophisticated borrowers."[212] Time to return, I guess, those "inclusivity" awards.

In *A Promised Land*, the "immaculately dressed" Dodd and his co-conspirator, Frank, emerge miraculously as the valiant pair that put their names on the Frankenstein's monster of "Wall Street reform" called the Dodd-Frank Wall Street Reform and Consumer Protection Act. At the time, both had been serving in Congress for twenty-nine years. Dodd, writes Obama, had become "pals with any number of industry lobbyists despite his liberal voting record." The phrase "due to" may be more apt than "despite." Lobbyists tend to want a slice of the government pie. Liberals like to dish it out.

In mid-July 2010, Obama signed Dodd-Frank into law. Throughout *A Promised Land*, Obama rarely shies from self-praise, but to call the passage of a bill that almost everyone has come to loathe "a significant triumph" suggests that his narcissism may have tipped from the metaphorical to the clinical. Although admitting the bill was riddled with "warts and unwanted compromises," Obama tries hard to convince his easily convinced audience that Dodd-Frank represented "the most sweeping change to the rules governing America's financial sector since the New Deal."[213] If "sweeping" means the same thing as "thoroughly and needlessly burdensome," Obama may have a point.

Obama's bizarre triumphalism is his way of denying that Trump totally owned him on Dodd-Frank. As subtle as a truck bomb, Trump called the law "a disaster" just ten days after his inauguration. "We're going to be doing a big number on Dodd-Frank," said Trump. "The American dream is coming back."[214] In *A Promised Land*, Obama provides no clue as to why Trump might have said this. In fact, he shares not a word from his critics. Among them was just about everyone who knew anything about finance, including New York City mayor, Michael Bloomberg.

In 2014, more than four years after the bill's passage, Bloomberg argued that in its attempt to regulate Wall Street Dodd-Frank ended up hurting Main Street. "The trouble is if you reduce the risk at these institutions, they can't make the money they did," said Bloomberg. "If they can't make the money they did, they can't provide the financing that this country and this world needs to create jobs and build infrastructure."

Bloomberg singled out the pitfalls of buying support. Bloomberg said, "What happens is every little group in Congress has to add something to that bill in return for their votes, and a lot of those things are just mutually exclusive. Years later now we don't have the regulations that are required and complying with it is just really impossible."[215]

In 2016, the US Chamber of Commerce spelled out the details of what it called a "regulatory nightmare." According to the Chamber, researchers had identified more than twenty-seven thousand new federal regulations linked to Dodd-Frank. These regulations were issued by some thirty-two distinct federal agencies and involved "more new restrictions than all other laws passed during the Obama administration put together." The Chamber worried that businesses would continue to struggle unless Congress alleviated these "onerous regulations."[216]

Although the Chamber leans right, in 2020 it endorsed twenty-three freshman House Democrats.[217] Bloomberg, of course, ran for president in 2020 as a Democrat. The conservative Heritage Foundation, feeling no need to play nice, called Dodd-Frank "one of the worst pieces of legislation ever passed by Congress." Heritage took particular aim at Obama's favorite feature of Dodd-Frank, the Consumer Financial Protection Bureau (CFPB).

The CFPB, argued Heritage, was a "regulatory nightmare," a phrase used so often in relation to Dodd-Frank it seems like a subtitle. Worse, the CFPB enjoyed "unprecedented power over the consumer financial market with almost no accountability to anyone." The DC Court of Appeals largely agreed, calling the CFPB leadership structure a "gross departure from settled historical practice."[218]

Never one for constitutional niceties, Obama deludes his audience into believing that "American families now had a powerful advocate in their corner."[219] More accurately, Obama might have said "some American families." In Obama's world, not all families were created equal.

In 2013, the CFBP, in league with Obama's Department of Justice, chose to go after Ally Financial, formerly known as GMAC. The CFBP decided that Ally was overcharging "minorities" in much the way mortgage lenders were alleged to have done. The problem for the Obama administration was that Ally did not keep racial data on its borrowers. To discern who was a minority, the CFPB had to make what the *Wall Street Journal* charitably called "educated guesses." This meant sending out 435,000 letters in the hope of finding the imagined 235,000 Ally "victims."

Using an algorithm based on addresses and names—DeShawn? Jesus? Barack?—the CFPB asked the recipients if they were, in fact, minorities. Those who claimed minority status—nothing sworn, nothing notarized—were entitled to a share of an $80 million settlement. "The CFPB and DOJ have carefully designed a process to reimburse consumers harmed by Ally's auto-loan pricing policies," CFPB spokesman Sam Gilford said. "There is a potential hitch," cautioned the *Journal*. "No one knows for certain whether all the people getting the checks will actually be minorities."[220] This is not the stuff of *1984*. It's the stuff of *Through the Looking Glass*.

The Old Camelot Magic

Among Christopher Dodd's many blessings, Obama tells us, is that he was "one of Ted Kennedy's best friends."[221] About Ted Kennedy, Obama cannot gush enough. The Kennedy Obama came to know was "the closest thing Washington had to a living legend."[222] In his early support of Obama's 2008 campaign, Kennedy was "was absolutely electric, summoning all the old Camelot magic, batting down the argument of inexperience once used against his brother and now directed toward me."[223] For the record, Ted's war hero brother, John, had served in Congress twelve years before launching his presidential campaign. Community organizer Obama had served two, and the toughest thing he ever fought were the waves at Waikiki.

Having risen from his deathbed to ensure the passage of Obamacare, Kennedy strikes Obama as worthy of canonization. The road to sainthood, however, must first pass across the bridge at Chappaquiddick. In the #MeToo era, not even progressives get to detour around it. An accounting of Kennedy's road to perdition may not belong in this memoir, but Obama should have factored it into his assessment of the man. The damage that Kennedy wrought on the women in his orbit—often with co-conspirator Dodd—did not end at that fabled bridge. In 1990, when journalists still felt some obligation to the truth, Michael Kelly wrote the following for *GQ*:

As [Carla] Gaviglio enters the room, the six-foot-two, 225-plus-pound [Sen. Ted] Kennedy grabs the five-foot-three, 103-pound waitress and throws her on the table. She lands on her back, scattering crystal, plates and cutlery and the lit candles. Several glasses and a crystal candlestick are broken. Kennedy then picks her up from the table and throws her on [Sen. Chris] Dodd, who is sprawled in a chair. With Gaviglio on Dodd's lap, Kennedy jumps on top and begins rubbing his genital area against hers, supporting his weight on the arms of the chair. As he is doing this, Loh enters the room. She and Gaviglio both scream, drawing one or two dishwashers. Startled, Kennedy leaps up. He laughs. Bruised, shaken and angry over what she considered a sexual assault, Gaviglio runs from the room.[224]

The incident above took place in 1985 at La Brasserie restaurant in Washington, DC, where Loh and Gavigilio both worked as waitresses. Obama may or may not have known of this at the time, but everyone in Washington did, and the story lived on. Obama surely knew about the Good Friday incident in 1991 when Kennedy commemorated the crucifixion by taking his nephew William Kennedy Smith and his son Patrick out barhopping. The young men brought two young women home with them. Hoping perhaps for his share of the action, a drunken Ted Kennedy, nearly sixty now, wandered without pants into the room where everyone gathered. The one woman fled in panic. The other woman claimed Smith raped her. Smith's criminal trial was long and very public. The Kennedys rallied to Smith's defense and cheered his acquittal.

To be fair, Obama does not discuss Trump's sexual peccadillos. He makes no reference in the book even to the infamous *Access Hollywood* tape. That job was left to every other Democrat on the planet, Michelle included. "I can't stop thinking about this. It has shaken me to my core in a way that I couldn't have predicted," Michelle said in November 2016 while stumping for Hillary in New Hampshire. "So while I would love nothing more than pretend that this isn't happening and come out here and do my normal campaign speech, it would be dishonest and disingenuous to just move on to the next thing like this was all a bad dream."[225] In her book, *Becoming*, she accuses Trump of "bragging" about "sexually assaulting women."[226]

As with almost everything questionable Trump has ever said, Democrats have magnified the words beyond their intent. Left out of Michelle's analysis of the *Access Hollywood* tape is one key phrase: "And when you're a star they *let* you do it. You can do anything." Sexual assault, of course, implies a lack of consent. Trump was no saint, but no one ever drowned in *his* Oldsmobile.

The only two references that Obama makes to sex of any kind in his book involve men whose public humiliation opened up political paths for Obama that might otherwise have remained closed. In 1995, Illinois Congressman Mel Reynolds was indicted for having sex with a sixteen-year-old campaign volunteer. His downfall set in process a series of events that led to Obama's becoming a state senator. The second man whose sexual appetites helped make way for Obama was Jack Ryan, Obama's formidable Republican opponent for the 2004 US Senate seat.

Obama writes, "The final blow came when the press got hold of sealed records from Ryan's divorce, in which his ex-wife alleged that he had pressured her to visit sex clubs and tried to coerce her into having sex in front of strangers."[227] Obama uses the phrase "the press got hold of" secure in the knowledge that his readers do not know or care how those records were gotten hold of. In 2007, even the *New York Times* took note of the talent Obama's people had for getting records unsealed, beginning with those of Obama's primary opponent in 2004, Blair Hull. The in-house fixer was chief strategist David Axelrod. "It is difficult to discuss Axelrod in certain circles in Chicago without the matter of the Blair Hull divorce papers coming up," wrote Ben Wallace-Wells of the *Times*. Hull had been leading in the polls until Axelrod's former employer, the *Chicago Tribune*, reported that during a divorce proceeding Hull's second wife had filed for a restraining order.

"In the following few days," Wallace-Wells continued, "the matter erupted into a full-fledged scandal that ended up destroying the Hull campaign and handing Obama an easy primary victory." The *Tribune* reporter who broke the story later admitted that the Obama camp "worked aggressively behind the scenes" to push the story. Many believe Axelrod, who had interviewed with Hull before signing on with Obama, actually leaked it.[228]

Having scored once with Hull, the *Tribune* filed suit in California to have Republican Jack Ryan's divorce records unsealed. Arguing that the public's right to know mattered more than potential embarrassment to the couple's nine-year-old son, Democrat Judge Robert Schnider overruled a court referee and ordered the records opened. Schnider, or so he said, wanted citizens to be "assured that there is no favoritism shown to the rich and the powerful."[229] In *Becoming*, Michelle describes the fact that both Hull and Ryan got "embroiled in scandals involving their ex-wives" as "lucky twists."[230]

One very good reason for Obama's discretion on matters sexual was the vulnerability of his heir apparent, former vice president Joe Biden. Beyond his public groping of little girls, Biden had one very serious charge of sexual assault hanging over his head. In April 2019, the story broke that in 1993 Biden had sexually harassed former staffer Tara Reade, who was twenty-eight at the time. In 1991, of course, Biden had chaired the Senate Judiciary Committee hearings that made Anita Hill a Democratic star and "sexual harassment" an office buzzword. Biden apparently didn't get the memo.

Reade hoped that the story of harassment was story enough to drive Biden out of a contested primary.[231] It wasn't. Party leaders were playing the long game. They needed a heterosexual who could be passed off as a moderate. That Biden was a serial sexual harasser did not much matter because the media would stay mum, and Trump was in no position to attack on the sex front.

In the fall of 2020, Reade told interviewer Alexis Daish the whole story. While a Senate staffer, Biden cornered Reade, forced her legs apart with his knee, whispered, "I want to f--- you," and penetrated her with his finger. When Reade resisted, Biden spat out, "You know, you're nothing to me, nothing." On October 4, 2020, the interview aired on *60 Minutes—60 Minutes Australia*, that is.[232] "The majority of news reporters probably fell at the more liberal end of the political spectrum,"[233] observes Obama. Well when a major news network offshores a killer story to Australia, there is no "probably" about it.

Unlike her American counterparts, Daish dared to address the issue of media bias. She acknowledged that Reade, unlike a Trump accuser, "faced a barrage of scrutiny." A lifelong Democrat, Reade agreed: "The fact that he was an elite Democrat put him in an untouchable position." As a result, said Reade, "I lost everything—work, legitimacy, reputation, friendships, housing—everything."

Biden deserved a 2017 humanitarian award for his efforts to protect victims of sexual violence as much as Obama deserved his Nobel Peace Prize. At the climax of his acceptance speech, Biden thundered, "No means no. Period. No matter when it's said. No matter how it's said."[234] In retrospect, the speech plays like some sort of grotesque parody, but the audience bought it. Today, most of his supporters remain as ill-informed as they were then.

If Michelle ever said anything about the Reade assault, I have been unable to find it. Reade's allegation apparently did not shake her to the core the way Trump's *Access Hollywood* tape did. In *A Promised Land*, of course, Obama says nothing about the incident either. He introduces Biden as "all warmth, a man without inhibitions, happy to share whatever popped into his head. It was an endearing trait, for he genuinely enjoyed people."[235] Obama likely knew the fix was in. He may well have overseen it, and no "elite Democrat" was more "untouchable" than Barack Obama.

I Make Love to Men Daily

Obama had one overriding reason for avoiding all discussion of sex, namely to mute talk about his own sexual orientation. Frank Marshall Davis, it should be recalled, was proudly bisexual. The poem Obama wrote in tribute to Davis, "Pop," contains provocative passages like the following: "Pop takes another shot, neat, Points out the same amber/ Stain on his shorts that I've got on mine, and/ Makes me smell his smell, coming/ From me…." Reviewers have found innocent ways to interpret this passage, but David Garrow's research suggests that they were avoiding the obvious.

In 2018, in the paperback version of his Obama biography, Garrow revealed an element of Obama's personality that had theretofore escaped attention at least by the media. Writing from New York to sometimes girlfriend Alex McNear in Los Angeles, the twenty-something Obama told McNear he viewed gay sex as "an attempt to remove oneself from the present, a refusal perhaps to perpetuate the endless farce of earthly life." Obama continued, "You see, I make love to men daily, but in the imagination. My mind is androgynous to a great extent and I hope to make it more so."[236] McNear was one of the editors of the Occidental literary review that published "Pop" a few years earlier.

This letter was not included in the hard cover edition of *Rising Star*, published in 2017. McNear had redacted the copy she shared with Garrow, thinking it "too explosive." A meticulous researcher, Garrow traced the original down to Emory University after McNear sold the letters, found the redacted passage, and added it to the paperback version.[237]

If this move seems bold, recall that in 2019 it was Garrow who risked his career, if not his life, to report a story that no American journalist wanted to hear, let alone report. The *New York Times* headline summed up the paradox: "His Martin Luther King Biography Was a Classic. His Latest King Piece Is Causing a Furor." The *Times'* Jennifer Schuessler reported, "While Dr. King's infidelities have long been known in broad outline, Mr. Garrow concludes by saying that the new material—including an explosive allegation that he witnessed, and even encouraged, a rape committed by a fellow minister—'poses so fundamental a challenge to his historical stature as to require the most complete and extensive historical review possible.'"[238]

That review was not forthcoming. The media and Garrow's peers were not remotely ready to submit King to the kind of #MeToo scrutiny other historical figures such as Thomas Jefferson or even John F. Kennedy faced, let alone the star chamber treatment Brett Kavanaugh endured a year before Garrow's 2019 revelations.

Obama is impressively safe on the #MeToo front. In *A Promised Land,* he claims that "lurid falsehoods" were being spread about him because of his "dark-hued" complexion including one that he "had fathered multiple children out of wedlock."[239] I have heard a thousand rumors about Obama, but I never heard that one. To his credit, there has been no Tara Reade lurking in his closet, no Monica Lewinsky. His memoirs are chaste to the point of prudish, if not exactly honest.

"I mean, there are several black ladies out there who've broken my heart,"[240] Obama tells his half-sister Auma in *Dreams,* but he is playing to his future constituents here. Neither Maraniss nor Garrow, both of whom looked hard, was able to identify a single black girlfriend except Michelle, and none has come forward.

In *A Promised Land*, Obama does not discuss his sex life. One would not expect him to. It is not that kind of memoir. In *Dreams from My Father*, he lumps three girlfriends, one of whom is of Asian descent, into what he would later admit was a white "composite." Garrow breaks it down. The Obama that Garrow sees through the eyes of these young women is remote, self-contained, and, in the eyes of Genevieve Cook, "ruthlessly ambitious."

Reflecting on Obama's ascent, Cook saw a man who papered over "a great deal of self-doubt" with "arrogance…some degree of self-glorification, and a strong dislike for being embarrassed, losing status, or having his reputation tarnished." At Obama's core, said Cook, was "a willingness to be insincere in order to bolster his need to be on top and in control…a personality where the need to win…trumps all the other stuff."[241]

Being no whiter than Obama, the half-Asian Sheila Jager resented being lumped into the composite. She told Garrow, "Our relationship was a tragedy that has weighed and haunted my life."[242] She explained the nature of the tragedy that befell both her and Obama. "I think the seeds of his future failings were always present in Chicago," Jager writes. "He made a series of calculated decisions when he began to map out his life at that time and they involved some deep compromises. There is a familiar echo in the language he uses now to talk about the compromises he's always forced to make and the way he explained his future to me back then, saying, in effect, I 'wish' I could do this, but pragmatism and the reality of the world has forced me to do that."[243]

I would argue that one of Obama's compromises was marrying Michelle. Another was living his life as a heterosexual. In 2020, Obama's sexuality would not be so touchy a subject save that in both *A Promised Land* and Michelle's *Becoming*, the Obamas paint a picture of married love that Hallmark would have thought excessive.

"Still, the smell of the ocean and sparkle of sunlight against the late summer leaves, the walks along the beach with Michelle, and the sight of Malia and Sasha toasting marshmallows around a bonfire, their faces set in Zen-like concentration—those things remained," writes Obama in one glowing portrait among many. "And with each day of extra sleep, laughter, and uninterrupted time with those I loved, I could feel my energy returning, my confidence restored."[244]

Obama has clearly come a long way from the guy who made love to men daily in his imagination. Perhaps like Elder McKinley in Broadway's

Book of Mormon, he learned to "turn it off, like a light switch." If so, he has overridden one of the bedrock principles of the LGBT movement, namely that sexual orientation is immutable.

If it seems a stretch to think Obama might be bisexual, consider the case of Andrew Gillum. In 2018, when Gillum won the Democratic nomination in the Florida gubernatorial race, he positioned himself as a stand-up family man. With his wife, Jai, and their three small children as a featured part of the campaign, Gillum came within a nose of winning the general election. In early 2020, serious people were considering Gillum, then a CNN contributor, as vice-presidential timber, especially if a white woman were at the top of the ticket. Then the wheels fell off the Gillum bandwagon. Did they ever.

In early March 2020, police found a naked Gillum sprawled on the floor of a Miami Beach hotel room littered with baggies of crystal meth. Sharing the room with him was an equally naked white male prostitute then in the throes of a drug overdose. "After conversation with my family and deep reflection, I have made the decision to seek help, guidance and enter a rehabilitation facility at this time," said Gillum. "This has been a wake-up call for me. Since my race for governor ended, I fell into a depression that has led to alcohol abuse."[245] From the photos at the scene, alcohol abuse would seem to be the least of the issues he would have to explain to Jai.

In September 2020 Gillum finally opened up. "I don't identify as gay, but I do identify as bi-sexual," said a soft-spoken Gillum to Tamron Hall in a TV interview. He added that this was not an admission he had ever before made in public.[246] In 2003, Benoit Denizet-Lewis, who is himself gay, wrote an eye-opening article for the *New York Times* magazine that helps clarify the pickle in which Gillum found himself.[247]

Denizet-Lewis described in detail the "Down Low" milieu in which Gillum moved and Obama may have. "Today, while there are black men who are openly gay," he wrote, "it seems that the majority of those having sex with men still lead secret lives, products of a black culture that deems masculinity and fatherhood as a black man's primary responsibility—and homosexuality as a white man's perversion."

A sophisticated "DL" underground emerged in the 1990s to accommodate black men like Gillum who were not prepared to go public with their proclivities. "If you're white, you can come out as an openly gay skier or actor or whatever," one man told Denizet-Lewis. "It might hurt you some, but it's not like if you're black and gay, because then it's like you've let down the whole black community, black women, black history, black pride." One can only imagine the culture pressure on a Gillum, let alone on an Obama, to maintain pretenses.

In *A Promised Land,* homosexuals are a "them." As a teenager, Obama confesses to using the occasional gay slur as adolescent males have likely been doing since the Bronze Age. In college, however, he met students and professors who were openly gay. He began, he claims, to understand "the loneliness and self-doubt that the dominant culture imposed on them." Obama writes, identifying himself with the dominant culture, "I felt ashamed of my past behavior—and learned to do better."[248]

Obama would do "better" on the LGBT question, yes, but not if it came at a cost. Among the "lurid tales" that he dismisses is that he "had worked as a gay prostitute."[249] I had not heard this rumor, but I was aware of the tale Larry Sinclair was telling. Obama surely was as well. Although never suggesting he paid for the service, Sinclair went on YouTube in January 2008 to discuss a two-day coke and sex romp he allegedly had with then-State Senator Obama in 1999 that sounds a whole lot like Gillum's 2020 misadventure. In May 2008 Sinclair upped the ante by staging a press conference at Washington's National Press Club.[250] For all his eccentricities and his petty rap sheet, Sinclair comes across as oddly believable. As a white man, he understood better than most how his accusation would be perceived. "All of a sudden," he said, "you're called a racist, a bigot."

Few people actually called Sinclair a racist because the media made sure few saw or even heard about the press conference. *Politico,* for instance, refused to publish Sinclair's "outlandish" allegations because they were "unsubstantiated." If Brett Kavanaugh ever reads this book, he will find *Politico*'s high-mindedness amusing. Obama ignores the Sinclair episode, which makes sense given that none of his fans will miss it.

The second LGBT-related omission from the 2008 campaign is harder to defend. In that few reviewers will catch the oversight, and fewer still will report it, Obama might be able to justify the omission as prudence. Prevarication comes closer to the mark. An honest memoir would include Obama's exchange with influential pastor Rick Warren at his presidential forum.[251] It was too consequential to ignore.

Given the audience at Warren's California megachurch, Obama played the role of pious Christian with brio. "I believe…that Jesus Christ died for my sins, and that I am redeemed through Him. That is a source of strength and sustenance on a daily basis," Obama told Warren. Cynics will not be surprised to learn that all mentions of Jesus or Christ in *A Promised Land* are incidental. If Christ remains a daily source of strength for Obama, he hides it well.

More to the point was Obama's response to Warren's question, "Define marriage." Said Obama for the ages, "I believe that marriage is the union between a man and a woman. Now, for me as a Christian, it's also a sacred union. You know, God's in the mix." Having left this exchange out of his book, Obama is free to ignore California's Proposition 8, the ballot measure that amended the state's constitution to define marriage as a union between a man and a woman. By failing to share his borderline—"God's in the mix"—blasphemy at Saddleback and his subsequent slighting of the LGBT cause, Obama negates the historical value of this memoir.

Two weeks before the November election, Warren endorsed Proposition 8. "This is one thing that politicians all tend to agree on," said Warren in a widely publicized video. "Both Barack Obama and John McCain—I flat out asked both of them—what is your definition of marriage, and they both said the same thing. It is the universal, historic definition of marriage, one man and one woman, for life."[252]

Excited by the Obama candidacy, African Americans in California (as elsewhere) turned out in record numbers on Election Day. An estimated 94 percent of them voted for Barack Obama and helped Obama carry the state with 61 percent of the vote. Moved in part by Obama's support of traditional marriage, an estimated 70 percent of blacks voted *for* Proposition 8, which carried the state with 52 percent of the vote. Black voters made that possible. Without them, Proposition 8 would not have passed.[253]

The UK *Guardian*, which routinely reported more honestly on things Obama than did their American counterparts, spelled out the LGBT reaction in its subhead: "California's reversal of gay marriage laws has infuriated the gay and lesbian community and spoiled the mood of celebration following Barack Obama's victory." One prominent blogger cited by the *Guardian* listed the many people he blamed for the proposition's passage, including the president and vice president-elect. "I'm angry with Barack Obama and Joe Biden," wrote Bill Browning, "for allowing their words to be used for anti-gay robocalls with their waffling on our relationships."

Browning was not the only angry gay Californian. "I am mad as hell and don't feel very chipper about Obama winning," said one commenter who understood Obama's history. "We will get nothing from him. He is weak and has shown in the past his readiness to throw those he doesn't need anymore under the bus i.e. Rev. Wright." Angered by the black vote but reluctant to slam black voters, one nimble white commenter on Browning's site eased his conflicted progressive soul by laying the blame not just "on white men as the root of all evil," but on their implicitly white urge "to infect [blacks] with Christianity."[254] So much for Gospel music.

Not until two years after the election did Obama publicly begin to rethink his position on gay marriage. "I also think you're right that attitudes evolve, including mine," he told one of a group of progressive bloggers he met with at the White House. "And I think that it is an issue that I wrestle with and think about because I have a whole host of friends who are in gay partnerships."[255] Soon enough, the word "evolve" became something of a punch line. When I put "Obama," "gay marriage," "evolve" into Google, I get 161,000 hits. *Ms.* magazine headlined its article on Obama's newfound support for same sex marriage in 2012, "Obama evolves!"[256] Everyone got the joke.

Everyone that is except Obama. It is well enough known how Obama had been evolving and devolving since he first came out in support of gay marriage as a state senate candidate in his progressive Chicago district in 1996. During that campaign, in fact, he wrote a letter to a local gay newspaper, declaring, "I favor legalizing same-sex marriages, and would fight efforts to prohibit such marriages."[257] Well known too is how he finessed his views for the next sixteen years to please his constituents and finally endorsed same-sex marriage only after Vice President Joe Biden blundered out his support ahead of schedule. Given his history, one would hope that Obama would address his use of the word "evolve" even as a humorous aside. He doesn't.

Above My Pay Grade

During Obama's appearance at Saddleback, Warren threw the candidate one more curve. Rather than ask Obama what his position was on abortion, the answer to which Obama had been finessing for more than a year on the campaign trail, Warren simply asked when do infants acquire "human rights." As a constitutional scholar, one whose only published piece in the *Harvard Law Review* dealt specifically with the civil rights of the unborn, this question should have been in Obama's wheelhouse. It wasn't. He whiffed, clumsily responding, "Answering that question with specificity, you know, is above my pay grade."[258]

Despite the fact that nearly eight million unborn babies would be denied their human rights during his tenure, more than two million of them black, Obama neglects the issue in his memoir. He fails to mention, for instance, that on just his third day in office he signed an executive order reversing Ronald Reagan's Mexico City policy, a ban on the funding of international organizations that provided abortions.

Only in one instance does abortion come into play and that is in regard to the passage of what Congress called the Patient Protection and Affordable Care Act (ACA). It was the Tea Party people, writes our prickly memoirist, who gave the ACA—an "abomination" in their eyes—the label "Obamacare."[259] Whatever its name, this was the bill closest to the president's heart.

Obama focused on health care from the beginning of his campaign. During his second debate with John McCain in 2008, Obama explained why the issue demanded attention. When asked by moderator Tom Brokaw whether health care was a right or a responsibility, Obama answered, "For my mother to die of cancer at the age of 53 and have to spend the last months of her life in the hospital room arguing with insurance companies because they're saying that this may be a preexisting condition and they don't have to pay her treatment, there's something fundamentally wrong about that."[260]

Obama was not the first politician to exploit the death of a relative for political gain—Al Gore and Joe Biden come quickly to mind—but few have done so as deviously as Obama. As Janny Scott of the *New York Times* revealed in her 2011 book, *A Singular Woman*, Ann Dunham's employer-provided health policy paid her hospital bills directly.[261] In *A Promised Land*, Obama dials down the mendacity. "I'd never forget my mother in her waning days," he writes, "fretting not just about her chances of survival but about whether her insurance would keep her solvent during treatment."[262] The actual "insurance" that worried Dunham was a disability policy she had signed up for after being diagnosed with uterine cancer. Cigna denied her claim. Obamacare did not address this peripheral issue in any case. Obama killed off his mother in vain.

In September 2009, Obama addressed a joint session of Congress to explain the wonders of the ACA. In the midst of the speech, a five-term congressman from South Carolina, Joe Wilson, shouted out, "You lie." This incident obviously got to Obama. He devotes two pages of his book to it. As Obama acknowledges, "Congressional criticism was swift and bipartisan." As to Wilson, he publicly apologized and called Obama to express his regrets, but Obama is still fuming. "They had demonized me," he writes, "and, in doing so, had delivered a message to all Republican officeholders: When it came to opposing my administration, the old rules no longer applied."[263]

One has to wonder here again how Obama could so thoroughly misinterpret his opposition. For eight years they walked on eggshells around Obama, which made Wilson's breach of decorum such an anomaly. In

2020, House Speaker Nancy Pelosi would rip up Donald Trump's State of the Union speech in full view of the cameras. Unlike the Republicans in 2009, no Democrat in Congress rushed to the microphones to apologize. Neither did Obama.

During this 2009 speech, Obama repeated the promise that would enable him to sell Obamacare, if not to the Republicans in Congress, at least to the wavering members of his own party. He had first introduced the theme in a June 2009 speech to a physicians' group. By the time of the ACA's passage, it had become Obama's mantra: "If you like your doctor, you will be able to keep your doctor. Period. If you like your health care plan, you will be able to keep your health care plan. Period. No one will take it away. No matter what."[264] This was not the lie that provoked Wilson, but it was a lie. Obama would repeat the same canard more than thirty times publicly. Politifact would later designate it as the "Lie of the Year."

In an honest memoir, Obama would have compressed all the tedious sausage-making details of the bill's passage and elaborated instead on the backstage drama that surely followed the exposure of this epic deception. He might have told us how he felt on hearing ACA architect Jonathan Gruber casually joke at a conference, "Lack of transparency is a huge political advantage. And basically, call it the stupidity of the American voter or whatever, but basically that was really, really critical for the thing to pass."[265] In this volume, Obama makes no mention of Gruber. Indeed, he makes no mention at all of his foundational promise, let alone its instant violation. Yet in dwelling on Wilson's challenge to his honesty, he calls attention to his lack of the same. Strange man.

Obama does touch on abortion but never on its morality. To ensure passage of the ACA in March 2010, Obama needed the support of the "devout Catholic" Bart Stupak, then a Michigan congressman, and his tiny caucus of pro-life House Democrats. They needed persuading. Despite Obama's earlier promises, the bill lacked a religious conscience clause or any language to prevent the federal funding of abortion.

Obama's message to Stupak and others was significant enough to deserve italics. "*This is it*," Obama claims to have told them. "*The point of it all. To have that rare chance, reserved for very few, to bend history in a better direction."* Inspired by Obama's plea, Stupak "worked with [Obama] on getting the abortion funding language to a point where he could vote for it."[266] That is the last readers hear of Stupak. The aftermath wasn't pretty.

The "funding language" in question was confined to an executive order that Obama never intended to honor. Stupak made the mistake of taking Obama at his word. As he soon discovered, he had helped bend history too far for the Right and not far enough for the Left. After three steady weeks of criticism from all sides, he announced he would not seek reelection.

In time, Stupak came to see just how badly he had been used. A Health and Human Services (HHS) mandate overrode the executive order and forced virtually all health plans, including those of religious institutions, to cover surgical sterilizations and abortion-inducing drugs. Stupak was dismayed. "Not only does the HHS mandate violate the Executive Order," he said two years after his pact with Obama, "but it also violates statutory law."[267] Obama was unfazed. For him, abortion was just a "wedge issue" pushed by "anti-abortion" activists whose "harsh moralizing" did not sit well with him or his constituents. Nowhere in the book does Obama spend so much as a paragraph reflecting on the ethics of an industry that killed, on his watch, nearly eight million future citizens.[268]

Readers will have to wait until the next volume to read about the botched rollout of Obamacare in 2013 and its subsequent failure to live up to any of its promises, especially the signature promise of keeping one's doctor and health plan. Obama leaves this chapter with a celebration of the bill's passage, a scratch behind his dog's ear, and thoughts about Ted Kennedy and his mom. "It was a good day."[269]

This Could Get Her Knocked off the Ballot

On the subject of sex, the aforementioned congressional pervert, Mel Reynolds, played a significant (if indirect) role in advancing Obama's career. In 1995, Reynolds made the rookie mistake of getting caught having a sexual relationship with a chatty sixteen-year-old campaign worker. This led to his indictment by a Cook County grand jury on criminal charges ranging from child pornography to obstruction of justice.

In Chicago, given that it takes an indictment to dislodge a sitting member of Congress, there was a Yukon-worthy rush to fill this open seat. A likely candidate was Alice Palmer, the state senator from Obama's district and something of a mentor to Obama. Like many of Obama's Chicago role models, Palmer had a history. In 1980, Prime Minister Maurice Bishop invited her to the workers' paradise of Grenada. There she attended celebrations commemorating the first anniversary of the Cuban- and Soviet-backed revolution that fundamentally transformed this tiny Caribbean nation. A few years later, she cofounded the Black Press Institute that provided a ready platform for members of the Communist Party USA. In 1985, four years before the fall of the Berlin Wall, she led a delegation of black journalists to the Soviet Union. In Obama's hipster neighborhood, the misadventures of this fellow traveler were résumé enhancers. [270]

Unfortunately for Palmer, Michelle Obama's family friend, Jesse Jackson Jr.—his sister was her maid of honor—also decided to file for the seat and bested Palmer in the primary. Like Reynolds, Jackson's congressional career scarcely made it past *Go*. In 2013, young Jackson was sentenced to thirty months in jail and his wife twelve months for supporting their lavish lifestyle with campaign donations. They also failed to report more than a half million dollars on their tax returns. This apple did not fall far from the Jackson family tree.

Having lost to the still untarnished Jesse Jr. in the primary, Palmer filed anew for her old Senate seat, and here is where things got sticky for Obama. "A few of her longtime supporters asked for a meeting, and when I showed up they advised me to get out of the race," he writes in *A Promised Land*. "The community couldn't afford to give up Alice's seniority, they said. I should be patient; my turn would come."[271] Obama ignored the pressure and continued his candidacy. It is hard to fault him. Palmer had made her support for Obama too clear too often for her to renege with any kind of grace.

The Palmer campaign was derailed even quicker than Blair Hull's or Jack Ryan's, and here too the Obama crew did the derailing. Palmer's weakness wasn't sex but signatures. "They're terrible. Worst I've ever seen," Obama quotes one of his backers as saying of the signatures on Palmer's petition to reenter the race. "All those Negroes who were trying to bully you out of the race, they didn't bother actually doing the work. This could get her knocked off the ballot."[272] A veteran of Project Vote, Obama knew a scam when he saw one. The problems he cites include invalid signatures, addresses outside the district, and multiple signatures with the same handwriting. Sound familiar?

"We've all been busting our asses out here, based on that promise," a female supporter tells Obama, referring to his promise to fight on. "And now, when she tries to screw you, and can't even do that right, you're going to let her get away with it? You don't think they would knock you off the ballot in a second if they could?"

The woman continues, "Naw, Barack. You're a good guy…that's why we believe in you. But if you let this go, you might as well go back to being a professor and whatnot, 'cause politics is not for you. You will get chewed up and won't be doing anybody a damn bit of good." Obama was convinced. Shocked by the obvious fraud, he challenged Palmer's petition. "Whatever vision I had for a more noble kind of politics," he said, "it would have to wait."[273]

In fact, Obama's people challenged the signatures of all four of his primary opponents. The Cook County Election Board spent a weary five days going signature-by-signature through the petitions. According to Garrow, a board member reported that "signatures were struck if they were obvious forgeries, if names were printed rather than signed, if the individual had listed an address outside the 13th Senate District, or if the individual was not registered at the specified address."[274] At the end of the review, the board declared all four of the opponents' petitions invalid. Obama ran unopposed.

This tale of dirty urban politics, illegitimate voters, enraged supporters, and a determined candidate so mirrors the reality of the 2020 election that this episode might have been edited out of *A Promised Land* had the book not already been shipped out by Election Day. To sustain the illusion that urban electoral politics were aboveboard in 2020, the media just had to ignore this inconvenient parallel.

Again, it is hard to fault Obama for contesting the fraudulent signatures of his opponents. As Obama well understood, Democratic politics have been ripe with fraud since Boss Tweed expanded the franchise to the dead a century and a half ago. Understanding fraud is one thing. Admitting it is another. Given his experience with urban election mischief, Obama's post-2020 election posturing left the knowing news watcher fighting one's spouse for the remote.

As always, the media were eager to enable Obama's piety. The first question the fawning Scott Pelley of *60 Minutes* asked Obama two weeks after the election was this: "What is your advice in this moment for President Trump?"[275] Pelley was referring to Trump's refusal to concede and his continued challenge to the posted results of the November 3 election.

Based on his own experience, Obama might have said, "If you let this go, you might as well go back to being a developer and whatnot, 'cause politics is not for you." Of course, he did not say that. What he did say was, "When your time is up, then it is your job to put the country first and think beyond your own ego and your own interests and your own disappointments." More specifically, Obama insisted that Trump should have conceded no more than two days after the election. The Democrats having gotten their man in, a more noble kind of politics was apparently back in vogue.

Although Pelley was interviewing Obama about *A Promised Land*, a book Pelley appeared to have read, neither of the two thought it prudent to revisit the 1996 state senate campaign, let alone Obama's sabotage of the Hull and Ryan campaigns. In the age of propaganda, it is hard to blame them. Nor, of course, did Pelley ask about the first four-figure donor to Obama's 1996 campaign, a developer named Tony Rezko.

If Pelley was mum on Rezko, Sarah Palin wasn't. When asked about Rezko during the 2008 campaign, Palin said, "It goes right back again to the candidate's judgment and who he chooses to associate himself with in the past, perhaps the present. It makes me question who he would associate himself with in the future."[276] Although Palin was blasted for questioning Obama's friends, Rezko was a legitimate target. As the *New York Times* conceded in May 2008, Obama admitted "he had made repeated lapses of judgment in dealing with an indicted Chicago real estate developer." He admitted, too, "Rezko had raised more money for his political campaigns than he had previously disclosed." In *A Promised Land*, Obama does not mention Rezko. In *Rising Star*, Garrow mentions him more than two hundred times.

My Shadowy Muslim Heritage

Although he has feinted at being both, Obama is no more a Muslim than he is a Christian. Playing Christian has been good for votes. Dabbling in Islam has been good for the ego. Throughout the memoir, he alludes to what he mockingly calls "my shadowy Muslim heritage" for no larger purpose than to showcase his own cosmopolitanism and to slam conservatives.[277] Secular to the core, Obama's true faith is "globalism," a word he uses only once in his book and then to mock his opponents. The word "globalist" does not appear at all. Obama prefers "internationalist," which, in his book, is a good thing.

Despite his secularism, Obama proved to be as sensitive to Muslim concerns, both at home and abroad, as he was insensitive to Christian ones. For all the words he dedicates to Muslim history, however, what comes across is how shockingly little he understands the faith he professes to respect.

In June 2009, Obama and his entourage tested their Islamic chops in Cairo. For some time, he and speechwriter Ben Rhodes, brother of then-CBS News President David Rhodes, had been working on what they called the "Muslim speech." As Obama tells the story, he insisted that the speech recognize "the extraordinary contributions of Islamic civilizations in the advancement of mathematics, science, and art."

Those contributions pale in comparison to those of Christian civilization, but there are no high-fives for Christianity anywhere. Obama also demanded that the speech spell out "the role colonialism had played in some of the Middle East's ongoing struggles." Obama tells the reader, as something of a boast, that he insisted on language "admitting past U.S. indifference toward corruption and repression in the region, and our complicity in the overthrow of Iran's democratically elected government during the Cold War, as well as acknowledging the searing humiliations endured by Palestinians living in occupied territory."[278] Obama stopped just short of apologizing for the "shores of Tripoli" line in the Marines' Hymn.

Obama reveled in his role as champion of the Islamic world. "As soon as I stepped onto the stage and delivered the Islamic salutation 'Assalamu alaikum,' the crowd roared its approval," writes Obama of his appearance at Cairo University. At speech's end, Obama bathed in "a prolonged standing ovation." In finding Rhodes afterwards, Obama deadpanned, "I guess that worked." Rhodes gushed, "That was historic."

The speech was more ahistoric than it was historic. Despite his lengthy disquisition on the faith, Obama does not begin to understand Islam. Mark Christian does. The son of Egypt's leading imam, Christian's deep dive into the roots of his faith caused him to abandon it. Upon learning his son's intention, Mark's father did what a Muslim true believer had to do: he tried to kill his son. Mark barely survived the bombing, fled to the United States, and converted to Christianity, changing his name along the way. Having helped Mark edit his book, *The Apostate*,[279] I know his story well.

In expressing the wish that the Saudis would see fundamentalism as "incompatible with modernity," Obama fails to grasp that "modernity" is just another word for Western civilization. Worse, the "gentler, more tolerant course"[280] he wishes on Islam is Western civilization at its most vulgar.

From his perspective, the model of what an Islamic country should look like is Indonesia. He speaks glowingly of "women riding Vespas in short skirts and high heels on their way to office jobs, boys and girls chasing kites, and long-haired youths dancing to the Beatles and the Jackson 5 at the local disco."[281]

Mark Christian sees this trend as a revived form of colonialism, now in its decadent phase. Egypt's Muslim Brotherhood, with which Mark is intimately familiar, rose up in reaction to the increasing sight of long-haired youths dancing to the Beatles. The "religious absolutism" that Obama deplores is simply Islam practiced the way Mohamed wanted it to be practiced. In encouraging Muslims to dilute their faith, Obama echoes the sentiments of colonialists past, but at least those hardy souls offered modern medicine, sanitation, electricity, indoor plumbing, and post-camel transportation as their part of the bargain.

Progressive imperialism offers the Islamic world little more than alien ideas and cultural rot. For those of us who wondered why the 9/11 terrorists would spend some of their last days partying at strip clubs, Christian has the answer. "In the video footage shown of the 9/11 hijack-ers one detail stands out," Mark writes. "None of these men who were about to perform jihad and die as a martyr looked angry. Rather, they seemed focused and relieved that they were about to be forgiven for all their sins, receive their rewards of heaven, and make eternal peace with Allah." Violent jihad purged the sins accrued by indulging in Western-style pleasures. The alternative for a believer was an eternal damnation more hellish than a mandatory course in white fragility.

On 9/11, the *jihadis* did not stray from their faith. They fulfilled it. In his defense of a proposed Muslim cultural center, dubbed "the Ground Zero mosque," Obama does not make this connection. Instead, he plays his Muslim card to the max with no apparent understanding of the game's rules.

In the summer of 2010, a group of families that had lost loved ones in the attack on the World Trade Center argued that to build a mosque within sight of the 9/11 memorial was, as Obama admits, "offensive to them and the memory of those who'd died in the World Trade Center at-tacks." This would seem a reasonable objection. Most Americans agreed. Had the Christian Identity movement decided to build a cultural cen-ter near the Murrah Building in Oklahoma City the Left would have screamed to its godless version of the heavens. "Nevertheless," writes

Obama, "right-wing commentators quickly seized on the [mosque] issue, often in nakedly anti-Islamic terms."

Obama decided to use the occasion of a dinner celebrating Ramadan to retaliate against the 9/11 families and their allies. Even by his own lofty standards, the self-righteousness on display here is impressive. "Last I checked, this is America," he claims to have told Chief of Staff Rahm Emanuel. "And in America, you can't single out one religious group and tell them they can't build a house of worship on their own property."[282]

True, the property had become more affordable after the landing gear of one of the doomed jetliners fell through its roof. True, too, the co-religionists of the mosque developers had been flying the jet that lost its landing gear, but why quibble when an opportunity to signal one's virtue so publicly presents itself. On the positive side, Obama's people did not dismiss the 9/11 massacre, as they did the 2009 Islamic terrorist attack at Fort Hood, as "workplace violence."

Throughout his presidency Muslims attacked and killed Christians with nary a word of reproach from the White House. In Obama's first year on the job, 2009, Muslims burned Christians alive in Pakistan. In 2010, Muslims massacred Coptic Christians in front of an Egyptian cathedral, killed more than one hundred Nigerians at a Pentecostal church, and targeted Christians in Iran with a wave of arrests. In 2011, a week after the killing of bin Laden, a Muslim assault on a Christian church in Cairo left a dozen dead. In *A Promised Land*, Obama speaks to none of these outrages—save for a brief mention of the bombing of a Coptic Christian church. Perhaps in the sequel he will tell us why his Department of Justice saw fit to scapegoat and subsequently imprison a Coptic Christian filmmaker for protesting such attacks.

Cairo was just one stop on what critics called Obama's "apology tour," a term he acknowledges but does not accept. "Evidently," he huffs, "my failure to lecture foreign audiences on American superiority, not to mention my willingness to acknowledge our imperfections and take the views of other countries into account, was somehow undermining."[283]

Conservative criticism unnerved Obama. He gripes, "It was another reminder of how splintered our media landscape had become—and how an increasingly poisonous partisanship no longer stopped at the water's edge."[284] Apparently, none of his editors reminded him that earlier in his memoir, he reminisces fondly about dismissing the war in Iraq as "dumb" before it even started.[285] That one evidence-free speech enabled him to garner progressive support in Chicago for his Senate run and later flank Hillary on the anti-war left.

From the moment the war in Iraq stalled, Obama and every other ambitious Democrat injected their "poisonous partisanship" into the debate. In January 2007, most of this crew reflexively denounced Bush's planned troop "surge," Obama among them. Said he at the time, "I am not persuaded that 20,000 additional troops in Iraq is going to solve the sectarian violence there. In fact, I think it will do the reverse." Although he would later admit that the surge "succeeded beyond our wildest dreams,"[286] his first instinct was to attack Bush, "the water's edge" notwithstanding.

I've Been Fighting
Alongside ACORN

I f Obama had one truly effective antagonist during his first term, it was the cheeky conservative provocateur Andrew Breitbart. Until his unexpected death in March 2012, no one posed more of a threat to the racial myths on which the Obama presidency sustained its power than the media-savvy Breitbart—not Donald Trump, not Sarah Palin, not the frequently cited Hannity and Limbaugh, and certainly not Boehner and McConnell. And yet in *A Promised Land*, Breitbart merits not a single mention, nor does the media enterprise that bears his name.

Working through his protégé James O'Keefe in 2009, Breitbart orchestrated the spectacular downfall of ACORN. This was the same ACORN about which Obama boasted in 2007, "I've been fighting alongside ACORN on issues you care about my entire career. Even before I was an elected official, when I ran Project Vote voter registration drive in Illinois, ACORN was smack dab in the middle of it, and we appreciate your work."[287] During the 2008 campaign, the dreaded Sarah Palin hung the ACORN albatross around Obama's neck, and Breitbart made it squawk.

Working off their credit cards and playing the roles of pimp and prostitute, the twenty-five-year-old O'Keefe and his twenty-three-year-old partner, Hannah Giles, covertly recorded ACORN staffers across the country. Almost without exception, the ACORN people proved eager to help O'Keefe find housing for his imagined stable of underage, illegal alien, sex workers. For Obama, the resulting videos were even more embarrassing than his girly-man opening day pitch at the 2014 Nationals' home opener.

The Census Bureau cut ties with ACORN. So did the Department of Housing and Urban Development. In his 2013 book *Breakthrough*, O'Keefe reveals what Breitbart thought to be Obama's Achilles' heel. "The president was not worried about ACORN's work in providing housing and tax services to the poor or our role in exposing this," writes O'Keefe. "He was worried about ACORN's pivotal role in harvesting and stealing votes and his own involvement therein. In the election fraud business, ACORN was General Motors, right down to the government subsidies."[288]

The raw power of O'Keefe's videos, amplified by Breitbart's media strategy, inspired John Boehner to introduce the "Defund ACORN Act." Although the Democrats controlled the House, the bill passed by a 345–75 vote margin with 172 Democrats voting in favor. The Democratically controlled Senate provided an even greater margin of victory, 83–7. Cornered, Obama had little choice but to sign a bill defunding an entity with which he was inextricably linked. Did I mention before there is not a word about ACORN in *A Promised Land*, or about Breitbart either?

Unlike Trump or Palin, both of whom preferred to avoid racial minefields, Breitbart pranced right in and through. A subversive bit of Democratic agitprop in March 2010 gave him the opportunity to show just how nimble he was. The occasion was a raucous Tea Party protest against Obamacare on Capitol Hill.

Democrats, Obama included, feared the Tea Party. Having grown used to manufacturing dissent, they had not seen a genuine, grass roots movement of such magnitude in the past half century. Obama even confesses to having "a grudging respect for how rapidly Tea Party leaders had mobilized a strong following."[289] That said, the Tea Party's "more troubling impulses" alarmed him. Yes, Virginia, those alleged impulses revolve around race.

"By September [2009]," Obama writes, "the question of how much nativism and racism explained the Tea Party's rise had become a major topic of debate on the cable shows."[290] The passive-aggressive Obama makes this observation as though the "cable shows" had some mission loftier than race-baiting conservatives. In any case, these talking heads set him to wondering, "Did that Tea Party member support 'states' rights' because he genuinely thought it was the best way to promote liberty, or because he continued to resent how federal intervention had led to an end to Jim Crow, desegregation, and rising Black political power in the South?"[291]

Having spoken to Tea Party groups across the country, I can assure Mr. Obama that a revival of Jim Crow was on no group's agenda. The Tea Party members old enough to remember Jim Crow correctly identified segregation with the Democratic Party. That fact alone made it anathema. Joseph Goebbels was a subtler propagandist than the leftists responsible for the recent explosion in the use of term "white supremacist." To his humble credit, Obama avoids that phrase and "white nationalist" as well.

If blind to the motives of Tea Party members, Obama could see the threat they posed to his reelection. Clearly, Obama loyalists picked up the vibes coming out of the White House. Still unclear is where these loyalists got their marching orders. What is undeniable is that almost immediately after the Tea Party emerged, the IRS began using its vast power to suppress it. In a predictably anodyne report issued in 2013, the inspector general of Obama's Treasury Department traced the beginning of the IRS crackdown to early 2010. As the report conceded, "The IRS used inappropriate criteria that identified for review Tea Party and other organizations applying for tax-exempt status based upon their names or policy positions instead of indications of potential political campaign intervention."[292]

In 2014, Tea Party organizer Catherine Engelbrecht testified before the House on what "inappropriate criteria" felt like at the ground level. No sooner did she file to incorporate her two groups than she found herself "a target of this federal government." Although neither she nor the business she ran with her husband had ever been audited before, in the next several years they would endure more than twenty audits or investigations by governmental agencies.

These audits occurred in addition to "the multiple rounds of abusive inquiries" she endured from IRS agents wanting to see all her Facebook and Twitter entries, the contents of her speeches, and the schedule of her speaking engagements. In concluding her testimony, Engelbrecht asked the committee "to end this ugly chapter of political intimidation."[293] In 2017, the Department of Justice settled with Engelbrecht and other Tea Party groups that had been protesting IRS abuse since 2010. The damage, however, had long since been done. The silencing of the Tea Party helped ensure Obama's 2012 reelection.

Obama mentions not a word of this abuse in *A Promised Land*. What he found noteworthy about Tea Party gatherings is that reporters "caught attendees comparing me to animals or Hitler." This admission provided one of the book's few laugh-out-loud moments, all inadvertent. Obama and his editors proofed this memoir four years into the Trump presidency. Did they not understand how *whiny* these complaints make Obama sound? Some anonymous Tea Party "attendee" compared him to Hitler? OMG! When I google "Trump Hitler," I get more than *forty million* hits.

Hell-bent on proving their own ignorant talking points, Congressional Black Caucus members tried to provoke Tea Party supporters during that Capitol Hill protest. They bypassed the tunnels they would normally take from the Cannon Office Building to the Capitol and waded through the crowd. Not getting the results he hoped for, Rep. Andre Carson improvised. Carson told reporters that he and Rep. John Lewis were "walking down the steps" of Cannon when they "heard 'n-word, n-word,' at least 15 times, hundreds of people."[294] Lewis chose not to comment. A veteran of the Selma marches, he had to understand that the tragic scenes of his youth were now being played out as farce.

Knowing his own allies, Breitbart refused to buy Carson's reckless slander for a second. In a risky bit of brinksmanship, Breitbart offered a one-hundred-thousand-dollar reward for any video showing a single person shouting a racial slur at any member of the Black Caucus, several of whom were recording the march as they walked. He got no takers. "What [the Democrats] did not expect was that new media would successfully challenge the propaganda of the old media and the Congressmen's racial smear," wrote Breitbart.[295]

Three months later, however, the NAACP resurfaced Carson's charges as if they had not been debunked. To counter the charges, Breitbart posted a video of United States Department of Agriculture (USDA) official Shirley Sherrod telling an approving NAACP audience how she had once discriminated against a white farmer.

Later in the same recorded talk, including the edited version posted by Breitbart, Sherrod told the audience how she had to assess her own bias and ended up helping the farmer. Within hours of its posting, however, Agriculture Secretary Tom Vilsack, with Obama's blessing, forced Sherrod's resignation. When the full story of Sherrod's remarks was revealed, a humbled White House offered Sherrod her job back and then some. None of this makes it into the pages of *A Promised Land*.

In investigating Sherrod, however, Breitbart stumbled on to a bigger story, *Pigford v. Glickman*, one whose absence from *A Promised Land* testifies to the memoir's inherent dishonesty. Starting in mid-2010, Breitbart pounded this story until his death in March 2012. The *New York Times* chose not to cover the case until after Obama was reelected, but the *Times* piece by reporter Sharon LaFraniere proved shocking in its candor.

Pigford v. Glickman was a complex lawsuit launched on the shaky premise that the US Department of Agriculture (USDA) unfairly denied certain black farmers USDA loans. In time, the case provided a fair warning of what reparations will look like if that madness ever comes to pass. Given that even the *Times* was willing to call *Pigford* "a runaway train, driven by racial politics, pressure from influential members of Congress and law firms that stand to gain more than $130 million in fees,"[296] the reader can imagine how corrupt *Pigford* really was. The *Times* estimated the total cost of the swindle at about $4.4 billion, in the words of one USDA analyst, "a rip-off of the American taxpayers."

Obama's fingerprints were all over *Pigford*. As a senator, he had supported expanding compensation. As president, he pressed for an additional billion or so to, as he might say, spread the wealth. For all the talk of social justice, the *Pigford* dollars proved to be little more than walking-around money for opportunistic Democrats. LaFraniere cited a black farm leader who told her that Obama's support for *Pigford* "led him to throw the backing of his 109,000-member black farmers' association behind the Obama presidential primary campaign."

Before the last dollar was handed out, just about every "marginalized" group in America had queued up for its slice of the action. Indeed, not since a tribe of Long Islanders convinced the Dutch they owned Manhattan had Indians come out so far ahead in a deal. A Berkeley professor who prepared a report on the case told LaFraniere, "It was just a joke. I was so disgusted. It was simply buying the support of the Native-Americans." President Biden did not launch the "racial equity" movement. The mania for racial equity drove the *Pigford* case, underscored the disastrous Consumer Financial Protection Bureau regulations, allowed ACORN to fester for decades, and caused the subprime crisis. A book could be written on the *Pigford* scandal—sorry, I forgot, the Obama administration was famously "scandal free"—but Obama does not even begrudge it a paragraph.

Obama ignores one other major issue in which Obama's DOJ appointees overruled career lawyers to appease Obama's base. Not surprisingly, this too had to deal with race. On Election Day 2008, two leather-jacketed members of the New Black Panther Party, one carrying a blackjack, threatened would-be voters at a Philadelphia polling location. When veteran civil rights attorney Bartle Bull approached him, he yelled, "Now, you will see what it means to be ruled by the black man, cracker!"[297]

In January 2009, the Bush Department of Justice filed a civil suit against three party members and the New Black Panther Party itself. Career DOJ attorney J. Christian Adams called the open intimidation by the Panthers "the simplest and most obvious violation of federal law I saw in my Justice Department career."[298] The law in question was the Voting Rights Act of 1965.

When none of the accused appeared in court to answer the charges, DOJ should have prevailed by default. In May 2009, however, Obama's appointees ordered Adams and his colleagues to stand down. "For the first time in our lifetime the power of the administration of the United States was working against the Voting Rights Act," said Bull. "They were protecting the people who were abusing the law."[299] Despite his much-bruited advocacy of voting rights, Obama let the suit die, no explanation forthcoming either then or now, not a word.

Fox News Conspiracy Theorizing

As Obama saw the world, and apparently continues to see it, those outside his orbit are consumed by race. Stirring those primal juices have been people like Sarah Palin, Donald Trump, Rush Limbaugh, and especially the luminaries at Fox News. Fox consumes Obama. The network strikes him as an un-American deviation from the nation's venerable media tradition, a tradition that once produced giants such as Walter Cronkite of CBS News.

For Obama, Cronkite was the gold standard of objective journalism, a man willing and able "to tell [voters] what was true." Obama refuses to understand, of course, that Cronkite was not in the truth-telling business. He was in the business of telling voters, under the cover of the news, what good liberals wanted to be true. In his review of Douglas Brinkley's friendly 2012 biography, *Cronkite,* Chris Matthews addresses "the elephant in the room"—the question of whether Cronkite was one of us, a liberal.

For Matthews, the question was a no-brainer. Of course he was. He cites Cronkite's constant worry that he would be outed: "I thought that some day the roof was going to fall in. Somebody was going to write a big piece in the newspaper or something. I don't know why to this day I got away with it."

Once retired, Cronkite could be more forthcoming. At a 1988 dinner honoring Democrat Congresswoman Barbara Jordan, he went full Howard Beale: "God Almighty, God Almighty, we've got to shout these truths in which we believe from the rooftops, like that scene in the movie 'Network.' We've got to throw open our windows and shout these truths to the streets and to the heavens." Cronkite made perfectly clear to this friendly crowd that "these truths" were liberalism's orthodoxies of the moment.[300] Everyone got the message, apparently, but Obama.

For the next twenty years, Big Media continued to move in the direction it had been moving in during the previous twenty years—leftward. CNN, NBC, CBS, ABC, PBS, NPR, Big Tech, the *Washington Post*, the *New York Times*, and the entire entertainment industry had become very nearly unified in their messaging. Obama was the beneficiary. Donald Trump was not.

By the end of the Trump presidency journalists no longer felt the need to hide their biases. In January 2021, Katie Couric made this leftward progression perversely clear. An heir to the Cronkite anchor chair and a past winner of the Walter Cronkite Award for her hit piece on Sarah Palin, Couric captured the newsroom zeitgeist with a remark so casually Maoist it would have made the Chairman himself blush. "They bought into this big lie," she said of Republicans. "And the question is how are we going to really almost deprogram these people who have signed up for the cult of Trump?"[301]

For four years Obama watched this ruthless collective attack the sitting president, and yet he still grieves about his treatment by the one major news outlet that challenged him. Obama writes, "I didn't believe a president should ever publicly whine about criticism from voters."[302] But ex-presidents? That's apparently a different story.

Like so many on the left, Obama overestimates the influence of Fox News. For the record, the network came on line in 1996 two years after Newt Gingrich's "Republican Revolution." For that matter, Ronald Reagan carried forty-nine states twelve years before Fox emerged and five years before Rush Limbaugh surfaced as a national figure. Conservatives never depended on a Walter Cronkite to tell them "the way it is" or ought to be. They have always had alternative media sources to ferret out the truth, their ever-adaptive samizdat.

As serious conservatives know and often lament, Fox has long been too mainstream for their tastes. So too were the Republicans in Congress who greeted Obama on arrival in 2009. One would not guess this from reading *A Promised Land*. Obama saw instead a Fox-driven "breed of Gingrich disciples, Rush Limbaugh bomb throwers, Sarah Palin wannabes, and Ayn Rand acolytes—all of whom brooked no compromise."[303] Time after time, Obama's failure to perceive the world as it is, willful or otherwise, renders his judgments delusional on arrival. Throughout the book, Obama overestimates not only Fox's influence but also its extremism. Rush Limbaugh long joked about the Left's perception of conservatives as "mind numbed robots." Obama gives life to that joke.

For him, Fox News is the robots' mothership, one whose business model "depended on making their audience angry and fearful."[304] This is a theme to which Obama returns repeatedly, calling Fox on another occasion "a network whose power and profits had been built around stoking...racial fears and resentments."[305] On still another occasion, he compares Fox to Al Jazeera in the way it fanned "the flames of anger and resentment," Al Jazeera among Arabs, Fox among white voters, in each instance with "algorithmic precision."[306]

In fact, it is Obama who scapegoats Fox News the way Al Jazeera does Israel. He does so to explain away his failure to get bipartisan support for any of his major proposals from the Stimulus to Dodd-Frank to Obamacare. He blames Fox for turning white conservatives against people "who didn't share [their] values, who didn't work as hard as [they] did, the kind of people whose problems were of their own making."[307]

In Obama's book, conservatives are always imagined as white. The fact that Trump got a higher percentage of the minority vote in 2020 than any Republican in sixty years had to break his fragile heart. As he sees it, opposition to the Obama presidency was inevitably race-based.

In one particularly unpleasant reflection, Obama wonders whether the race of his attorney general, Eric Holder, made him "the favorite target in my administration for much of the Republican vitriol and Fox

News conspiracy theorizing." Holder seemed to think so. Obama writes, "'When they're yelling at me, brother,' Eric would say, patting my back with a wry smile, 'I know they're thinking of you.'"[308] The brothers delude themselves. Fox News viewers know more about Holder than Obama appears to. They certainly know better than to write, as Obama did, that Holder had just "one blemish" on an "otherwise spotless record."[309]

I Instructed Hillary

Although nearly two thousand American military personnel would die in action on Obama's watch, the fate of no serviceman concerned him more than that of an unnamed weapons officer whose F-15 crashed in Libya in March 2011. As Obama tells the story in *A Promised Land*, he worried so much about the man's safety he could not enjoy the sumptuous dinner he was sharing with his host, the president of Chile. Obama writes, "All I could think about was the young officer I had sent into war, who was now possibly injured or captured or worse. I felt as if I might burst."[310]

Despite his Nobel Peace Prize, Obama's concern was not exactly humanitarian. The prior year, 2010, had been the deadliest in America's then-nine-year engagement in Afghanistan. Nearly five hundred Americans were killed in that hellhole alone. What worried Obama about the F-15 officer was that America's support for his misadventure in Libya was so tenuous a single American death could undo it.

To Obama's temporary good fortune, the man was rescued. Without congressional authorization, the mission continued. Obama brags that his passive-aggressive "lead from behind" role in the NATO takedown of Libya strongman Muammar Gaddafi resulted in "the quickest international military intervention to prevent a mass atrocity in modern history."[311] In the Obama calculus, an atrocity prevented is the military equivalent of a job saved, each worthy of a boast but neither capable of being verified. In the case of Libya, however, evidence strongly suggests that Obama was working off a false premise: the "bloodbath" he repeatedly promised was never in the cards. Unlike Iraq's WMD threat, contrary evidence was available before the intervention.

In his March 28, 2011, address to the nation justifying the attack on Libya, Obama claimed that if America had delayed just one more day, "Benghazi, a city nearly the size of Charlotte, could suffer a massacre that would have reverberated across the region and stained the conscience of the world."[312] Two weeks later, Alan Kuperman, a professor of public affairs at the University of Texas and author of *The Limits of Humanitarian Intervention*, did the math Obama still refuses to do. Writing in the *Boston Globe*, Kuperman made the simple point, "The best evidence that Gaddafi did not plan genocide in Benghazi is that he did not perpetrate it in the other cities he had recaptured." In Misurata, a city of four hundred thousand retaken by Gaddafi's forces, only 257 people were killed in two months of fighting. Moreover, cell phone cameras failed to capture any images of a massacre.

As Kuperman explained, rebel forces did what rebel forces have been doing since the dawn of the age of mass media: they faked a humanitarian crisis to save their futile cause. Kuperman had no reason to embarrass Obama.[313] A Democrat, he had previously served as legislative director for then Congressman Chuck Schumer.

Gaddafi, for all his despotic flaws, had recently abandoned his WMD program and his terrorist arm. Obama admits as much. "It's fair to say that I found the idea of waging a new war in a distant country with no strategic importance to the United States to be less than prudent,"[314] he writes. Readers curious about why he intervened, if not to prevent a Rwanda-sized stain on his legacy, may have to wait for Volume II of the memoir. This volume ends with Osama bin Laden's death in May 2011. The unraveling of Libya that leads to September 2012 attack on the Benghazi consulate goes unreported.

Although Obama and his party relentlessly criticized the Bush administration for its failure to anticipate conditions in post-Saddam Iraq, Obama did arguably worse in Libya after the fall of Gaddafi. Although he spares readers the details in this volume, he appears to be setting Hillary Clinton up to take the fall.

A Promised Land might be worth buying if Obama were honest about his relationship with Hillary. He isn't. In explaining why he chose Hillary to be secretary of state, he dismisses the "various theories" about the pick and asks the reader to believe, "I thought Hillary was the best person for the job." In addition to her intelligence and her work ethic, he fixes on Hillary's "star power." This, he believes, would help her repair relationships that allegedly deteriorated during the Bush years.[315]

Yet for all the "bandwidth" Hillary added to Obama's foreign policy team, he is forever either telling her what to do—as in, "I instructed Hillary to call Netanyahu and let him know I wasn't happy"[316]—or writing her out of the picture—as in, "[Medvedev] expressed enthusiasm for our proposed 'reset' of U.S.- Russia relations."[317] A more secure memoirist would have "asked" her, not instructed her, and given her credit for the reset policy with which she is publicly identified.

Libya, by contrast, represents the rare instance in which Obama grants Hillary full agency over her actions. The triumph was his. The ensuing mess was hers. "According to the U.S. diplomat Hillary had sent to Benghazi to act as a liaison to the emerging governing council there," he writes, "the opposition was at least saying all the right things about what a post-Gaddafi Libya would look like, emphasizing the importance of free and fair elections, human rights, and rule of law." Take note: *Hillary* sent the diplomat. Obama follows this passage with what may be the lowest blow in a book filled with unseemly punches. As the saying goes, dead men tell no tales:

> "Who is it that we sent to Benghazi?" I asked, after hearing one of these dispatches.

> "A guy named Chris Stevens," Denis [McDonough] told me. "Used to be chargé d'affaires at the U.S. embassy in Tripoli, a bunch of Middle East posts before that.

Apparently, he and a small team slipped into Benghazi on a Greek cargo ship. Supposed to be excellent."

"Brave guy," I said.[318]

Obama will have a lot of explaining to do in *A Promised Land II*. He might profitably begin by answering two questions few in the American media have dared ask him, one complex, one very simple. The complex one deals with Stevens's mission. Was Stevens sent to Libya to buy back Stinger missiles issued by Hillary's State Department to al-Qaeda groups? The simple question no one has posed directly to the president: What exactly did *you* do on the night of September 11, 2012?

More generally, Obama will also have to address the charges that former Democratic Senator Joe Lieberman leveled in a stinging *Washington Post* op-ed from February 2016. "The simple fact is that there is more instability in the world today than at any time since the end of World War II," wrote Lieberman. "The threats come from emboldened expansionist powers such as Iran, Russia and China, and also terrorist aggressors such as the Islamic State and al-Qaeda. In short, the enemies of freedom are on the march." When asked what America can do to best help him and his country, a European ally told Lieberman, "Elect a president who understands the importance of American leadership in the world."[319] And that is exactly what America did.

Apache Helicopters Leveling Entire Neighborhoods

Some words give away the game. One such word is "stunt." In *A Promised Land*, Obama uses the word multiple times, usually as a criticism of some transparently political campaign gambit that has gone awry, for instance, "Reporters saw McCain's latest move for what it was: a hasty retreat after a political stunt that had backfired."[320]

In using the word "stunt" to describe the September 2000 visit by Likud leader Ariel Sharon to Jerusalem's Temple Mount, Obama shows his hand. For those readers who need confirmation of his bias, he describes the Temple Mount as "one of Islam's holiest sites" and neglects to mention that for Jews the Temple Mount is *the* holy site as well as the historical locus of their history as a people. By contrast, Mohamed's only visit came on the back of Buraq, the beautiful white man-beast who flew him to Jerusalem through the night skies and got him back home to Mecca in time for his morning joe.

As he does nowhere else in the book, Obama provides a lengthy history of the international conflict under study. The problem, as Israeli writer Dov Lipman reported, is that Obama's history "not only exhibits a flawed understanding of the region—which clearly impacted his policies as president—but misleads readers in a way that will forever shape their negative perspective of the Jewish state."[321]

The views of American-born Lipman, a member of the centrist Yesh Atid Party, reflect those of Jews across the political spectrum save, of course, for those on the hard left. Sean Durns, senior research analyst for the Committee for Accuracy in Middle East Reporting in America (CAMERA), wrote, "Barack Obama both ignores and omits key facts about the Middle East. In particular, the former president gets relevant Israeli history wrong."[322] In an otherwise positive review of *A Promised Land* in the *Jerusalem Post*, Gil Troy observed that Obama's "European-style obsession with power dynamics and America's lack of exceptionalism made him too indulgent of the sins of dictators and terrorists like the Iranians and the Palestinians, and too harsh regarding the missteps of liberal democrats like the Israelis."[323]

From the very beginning, Obama has swam with the current of anti-Zionist, post-colonial sentiment coursing through the international Left. "I chose my friends carefully," Obama writes of his college days in *Dreams*. He and his friends discussed "neocolonialism, Franz [*sic*] Fanon, Eurocentrism, and patriarchy." In Chicago, one of Obama's best friends was Rashid Khalidi, a Palestinian-American scholar and a one-time shill for the Palestinian Liberation Organization (PLO). David Garrow writes matter-of-factly about "Barack and Michelle's attendance at the almost nightly dinners at the Khalidis' or Bill Ayers and Bernardine Dohrn's home" as though this were common knowledge. It wasn't, at least not on the campaign trail in 2008.[324]

Obama's friendship had the potential to derail that campaign. In 2003, he attended a going-away party for Khalidi, who was leaving Chicago for a job in New York. The *Los Angeles Times* acquired a copy of the video shot at the party. Although the *Times* reported some of the toasts offered to Khalidi—including an anodyne one by Obama and another that compared "Zionist settlers" to Osama bin Laden—its editors refused to air or share the tape. As a close friend to both Obama and Khalidi, Bill Ayers might have had an interesting moment or two of his own. If so, the world still doesn't know.

To succeed at the national level, a Democrat cannot appear to be openly anti-Semitic or aggressively anti-Israel. Obama understands this.

In *A Promised Land*, he takes pains to establish that although he may be pro-Palestinian, he is not anti-Semitic. He now insists he read Frantz Fanon only to impress a would-be girlfriend and mentions "activist and Middle East scholar" Khalidi just once and in passing.[325]

In an argument that sounds an awful lot like, "But some of my best friends are Jewish," Obama writes that in high school he "devoured the works of Philip Roth, Saul Bellow, and Norman Mailer." Precociously intersectional, Obama claims to have been "moved by stories of men trying to find their place in an America that didn't welcome them."[326] I will believe that Obama might have "devoured" Roth in high school, at least *Portnoy's Complaint*. Lots of horny adolescents did. But are we really supposed to believe that the same indifferent student who "didn't discuss much beyond sports, girls, music, and plans for getting loaded" voluntarily read Saul Bellow?[327]

If Obama's anti-colonial posturing is fairly shallow, he has a heartfelt distaste for the political right, a force that concerns him only in Israel and in the United States. He never applies the term "right" to Muslims and/or Arabs, no matter how conservative their values might appear to the American Left.

In Obama's retelling, the Oslo Accords were undone by the "far-right Israeli extremists" who assassinated Israeli Prime Minister Yitzhak Rabin. "Liberal" Shimon Peres succeeded Rabin but lost in a snap election to Benjamin "Bibi" Netanyahu, "the leader of the right-wing Likud party."

Defeated in 1999, Netanyahu was on the sidelines when Sharon's "stunt" at the Temple Mount "enraged Arabs near and far" and helped trigger the Second Intifada. As Obama relates the story, a minor masterpiece of moral equivocation, "stone-throwing protestors" kicked off four years of violence that culminated with "U.S.-supplied Israeli Apache helicopters leveling entire neighborhoods."[328] Wrote Lipman of this accusation, one that also implicates the United States, "What does [Obama] mean by 'leveling entire neighborhoods,' other than to imply that Israel indiscriminately bombs Gazan neighborhoods, willfully murdering innocent people? And what human being on Earth wouldn't be riled up to condemn Israel for such inhumane activity?"[329]

By the time of Obama's inauguration, Netanyahu had returned to power. Obama pointedly describes him as having a "gray comb-over," a subtle indicator of a capacity for deceit that, from Obama's perspective, Netanyahu will repeatedly exercise. More to the point, Bibi, like Sarah Palin and Jesse Jackson, has an air of authenticity that seems to intimidate Obama. As he all but confesses, he can never be the alpha male Netanyahu clearly is.

According to Obama, Bibi "inherited his father's unabashed hostility toward Arabs" and "built his entire political persona around an image of strength." His tough guy stance attracted the "most hawkish" members of the American Israel Public Affairs Committee (AIPAC) and "wealthy American right-wingers." Like American right-wingers, Netanyahu doesn't promote healthy debate. He orchestrates "noise," noise that distracts Obama from his noble goals.

Despite Israel's dependence on American largesse, Netanyahu refused to play supplicant. He not only defied Obama's request to restrict new settlements, but he also dared to announce the granting of new housing permits in East Jerusalem during a Joe Biden visit. The move prompted Obama to "instruct" Hillary to make her call. His macho posturing here covered his own fear of confronting Bibi. Later that month the still defiant Netanyahu told an AIPAC gathering in Washington, "Jerusalem is not a settlement—it is our capital."[330]

In the run-up to the 2010 midterms Obama hoped to hammer out a peace deal to bolster his party's faltering chances. Sensing the desperation, Netanyahu refused to yield. In one of the rare such concessions in *A Promised Land*, Obama admits he did not succeed. Fortunately, he has an Israeli deplorable to blame. Netanyahu, Obama writes, "refused to extend the settlement freeze" and "was threatening to make life harder for the Palestinian Authority."[331] The nerve!

To get a sense of how far Obama strays from the facts in telling the story of Israel's past and present, it would pay to read Lipman's account in the *Jewish Press*. "I surely would have expected truth, accuracy and fairness from Barack Obama, America's 44th president," lamented Lipman, who never previously criticized Obama in public. "But the falsehoods and inaccuracies in this memoir only feed the theory that Obama was, in fact, anti-Israel. Now, through *A Promised Land*, he seeks to convince others to join him."[332]

As Obama might say, "Ouch."

We're Gonna Punish
Our Enemies

In each election cycle, Democrats, especially suburban Democrats with guilty consciences, signal the progressive virtue du jour on their yard signs. In 2020, it was all "Black Lives Matter" and "Racism Is a Sin." In 2018, it was "Keep Families Together" and "Children Belong on Playgrounds NOT in Cages." The assumption underlying these signs in 2018 was that the orange-haired scoundrel in the White House had made it his demonic goal to rip children from the arms of their immigrant parents and throw them into cages.

In his memoir, Obama makes an unexpected admission. In attempting to explain why his party was about to lose sixty-three seats in the House in the 2010 midterms, he cited the pushback he was getting on the campaign trail from "activists"—remember, there are no left-wingers in *A Promised Land*. Obama writes, "Young Hispanics asked why my administration was still deporting undocumented workers and separating families at the border." [333]

With this admission Obama's more sensitive readers had to brace themselves from fainting: *You mean Obama's people separated families at the border?* Yes, they did. Not only that, but Obama failed to do what President Trump did in 2018, namely sign an executive order reversing the policy. Those who placed the mournful yard signs in 2018 were protesting a practice that had been standard practice under Obama and halted more than four months before the election. Obama makes no mention of the "cages" in the book, but as the *Washington Post* conceded in an October 2020 headline: "'Kids in cages': It's true that Obama built the cages at the border."[334]

Obama admits as well that his administration "was deporting undocumented workers at an accelerating rate." The "undocumented" euphemism we have grown used to. The phrase "undocumented workers" stretches the euphemism beyond recognition. The deportation of "workers" was not accelerating, but the deportation of "undocumented immigrants with criminal records" most certainly was.[335]

Deporting criminal aliens would seem a good thing to most Americans, even to most Democrats in that they voted to authorize the policy. Not to Obama. He introduces this passage with the phrase, "Worse yet." Being a progressive takes work. Obama has to constantly amend his own history to keep pace with the yard signs.

Ever inclusive, Obama believed in defining the "American family" broadly. In this otherwise carefully edited book, his definition of the family would get a fat "F" in taxonomy class: "It included gay people as well as straight, and it included immigrant families that had put down roots and raised kids here, even if they hadn't come through the front door." Let's see, we have moved from "land of the free and home of the brave" to "land of gays and straights and home of immigrants, legal or otherwise." That about sums up Obama's huddled masses.

Obama's "family" had no room for Republicans, at least not those who opposed Obama's ideas on immigration reform. He made this clear in October 2010, urging Latino voters to head to the polls with one idea in mind: "We're gonna punish our enemies, and we're gonna reward our friends who stand with us on issues that are important to us."[336]

In October 2020, the media and Big Tech would have blocked the reporting on the "enemies" story. In October 2010, Obama's unwitting honesty could still make news, and that news hurt his party's cause. In imagining "Latinos" as a racial voting bloc, he shed a little too much light on the Democrats' long-term strategy of turning illegal aliens into

Democratic voters. A more candid memoirist would have discussed that strategy. In *A Promised Land*, Obama does not even mention the gaffe, not even to protest the conservative shorthand for illegal border crossers, "undocumented Democrats."

Despite the Democrats' control of both houses during his first two years as president, Obama passed no meaningful immigration legislation. After the 2010 midterm, he tried to ram the DREAM act through Congress before those ill-fated, sixty-three House members evacuated their Cannon Building offices, many for lobbying firms nearby, but he had no luck with that either.

The failure of the Democrats to hold the House made Obama question the democratic enterprise. After all, he writes with an alarming lack of modesty, he and his colleagues had "gotten more done, to have delivered more significant legislation that made a real impact on the lives of the American people, than any single session of Congress in the past forty years."[337]

Soon after the defeat, while traveling in India and reflecting on the rise of factions like America's Tea Party, Obama had a minor epiphany. "I found myself asking," he writes of the midterm disaster, "whether those impulses—of violence, greed, corruption, nationalism, racism, and religious intolerance, the all-too-human desire to beat back our own uncertainty and mortality and sense of insignificance by subordinating others—were too strong for any democracy to permanently contain."[338] To get his way, he would simply have to end-run democracy.

As late as March 2011, Obama was still playing by the rules. He explained at a Univision town hall why he could not help the "Dreamers"—young people brought to this country illegally by their parents. "America is a nation of laws," he said, "which means I, as the President, am obligated to enforce the law. I don't have a choice about that." Obama was very specific about which laws he was obliged to enforce. "With respect to the notion that I can just suspend deportations through executive order, that's just not the case, because there are laws on the books that Congress has passed."[339]

In Volume II Obama will explain how he decided to ignore the laws on the books and custom design an immigration policy "more fair, more efficient, and more just" than Congress ever could.[340] All it took to counter the Tea Party's nativism and racism, he now realized, was a stroke of the presidential pen. The media wouldn't protest his brash override of the Constitution—certainly not with an election looming and countless Hispanics primed to punish their enemies.

Wandering a Cracked Earth

In the fall of 2019, three years out of the White House, Barack Obama signed the papers for a nearly seven-thousand-square-foot, waterfront home on Martha's Vineyard, a short bicycle ride from Chappaquiddick. He may not have led the Joshua generation anyplace useful, but he sure as hell found his own promised land.

The Obamas paid nearly twelve million dollars for the property. No big deal. They had money to spare, having received a reported sixty-five-million-dollar advance for their respective memoirs from Penguin Random House.

In his memoir Obama worries that he did not do enough to deal with "America's escalating inequality." He wonders whether he should have attempted "to exact more economic pain" in the short term in the hope of creating a more just economic order. "The thought nags at me," he insists. That thought might have nagged him a little less had he bought a three-bedroom cottage on Lake Michigan and spread the excess wealth around.

Back at Martha's Vineyard, Obama enjoyed a glorious view of a barrier beach and the ocean beyond. This might have soothed the troubled soul of the ordinary parvenu, even a socialist one, but for Obama the view fueled still another anxiety. Although Big Media were predictably mum about the irony of his purchase, the samizdat relished it. "Geez, he really did stop the oceans," wrote one wry blogger in a headline Obama totally deserved.[341]

The blogger was referring to an Obama-brag much better known in conservative circles than in liberal ones. In his speech celebrating his capture of the 2008 Democratic nomination, Obama registered a Louis XV-like score on the hubris spectrum. If the French king promised a deluge with his departure, Obama promised exactly the opposite with his arrival. "I am absolutely certain," he told the assembled masses, "that generations from now we will be able to look back and tell our children that this was the moment…when the rise of the oceans began to slow and our planet began to heal."[342] He was certain that many other wonderful things would happen with his nomination, but the ocean rising line proved to be something of a high-water mark.

Although the quote does not make it into *A Promised Land*—no surprise there—what does surprise is Obama's near obsession with climate change. Other than race—understood—no other issue affects him quite as viscerally as does the climate. Despite the purchase of his seaside home a year before the book was published, Obama does not ease the reader's anxiety about the apocalypse to come. Indeed, Puritan divines went easier on their audiences than Obama does on his. Consider the following two passages, best experienced unedited:

> By the time I was running for president, the clear consensus among scientists was that in the absence of bold, coordinated international action to reduce emissions, global temperatures were destined to climb another two degrees Celsius within a few decades. Past that point, the planet could experience an acceleration of melting ice caps, rising oceans, and extreme weather from which there was no return.[343]

In this second passage, his Jeremiad expands from mere warming and rising seas into total, balls-to-the-wall catastrophe. Rachel Carson could not have been more hysterical:

But the best estimates involved a hellish combination of severe coastal flooding, drought, wildfires, and hurricanes that stood to displace millions of people and overwhelm the capacities of most governments. This in turn would increase the risk of global conflict and insect-borne disease. Reading the literature, I pictured caravans of lost souls wandering a cracked earth in search of arable land, regular Katrina-sized catastrophes across every continent, island nations swallowed up by the sea. I wondered what would happen to Hawaii, or the great glaciers of Alaska, or the city of New Orleans. I imagined Malia, Sasha, and my grandchildren living in a harsher, more dangerous world, stripped of many of the wondrous sights I'd taken for granted growing up.[344]

About the only concern Obama doesn't express is the fear that Hawaii—Google "Hank Johnson Guam"—might capsize. Yet despite these fears, Obama somehow found the courage to buy a seaside estate that gobbled at least three times the energy of the average American home. The purchase calls to mind another memorable quote from a doomed French royal, "*Qu'ils mangent de la brioche.*" Let them eat cake.

Obama went coastal despite his admitted failure to create a "bold, coordinated international action to reduce emissions" and despite President Trump's withdrawal from the Paris Climate Accord. One would think that just for appearance's sake the Obamas would have bought a house, if not in his imagined Kansas homeland, at least a few miles inland. But no, the Obamas have never really had to worry about appearances.

The beachfront purchase would seem to make Obama not just a hypocrite, but worse, a "climate change denier," the unholy label he pins on Czech president Václav Klaus.[345] Among the few to explain the provenance of this slur was Pulitzer Prize–winning columnist Ellen Goodman. "I would like to say we're at a point where global warming is impossible to deny," Goodman wrote in 2007. "Let's just say that global warming deniers are now on a par with Holocaust deniers, though one denies the past and the other denies the present and future."[346] Obama had to know the word's source. Whether he knew that Klaus had grown up during the Nazi occupation of Czechoslovakia I cannot say.

In 2007, however, Goodman was still using the phrase "global warming." It would remain the term of art for a year or two before the phenomenon would subtly be rebranded as "climate change." There was a reason for the shift in semantics. By 2011, when Obama's memoir concludes, the earth was in the thirteenth year of what even activists admitted was a "global warming hiatus," a period in which the earth did not warm.[347] Obama neither explains the language shift nor the rationale behind it.

For anyone paying attention, the hiatus exposed the weakness of the computer models and made Obama's apocalypse all that much harder to peddle. Even though the hiatus would have helped excuse his poor salesmanship, Obama never speaks of it. Nor does he write about the news that undermined his personal participation in the December 2009 UN global summit on climate change in Copenhagen.

Two months earlier Obama had flown to Copenhagen to pitch Chicago as the site for the 2016 Olympics. "President Obama not only failed to bring home the gold," wrote the *New York Times*, "he could not even muster the silver or bronze."[348] Although he does not address this minor humiliation in his memoir, he does reflect on the optics of air travel. "Has anyone ever considered," he asks an aide on the flight to the Copenhagen summit, "the amount of carbon dioxide I'm releasing into the atmosphere as a result of these trips to Europe?" The aide joked, "You might not want to mention that in your speech tomorrow."[349]

Obama pours an excessive amount of ink—he writes longhand, remember—into this summit and the unhappy history leading up it. "You know things have hit a low point when our closest allies think we're worse on an issue than North Korea," an adviser tells him.[350] Obama comes to Copenhagen to right that history, but he cannot bring himself to explain one of the major reasons why the summit failed.

In its opening sentence, a *Politico* article spelled out the problem: "'Climategate' has muddied the good green message that was supposed to come out of the United Nations climate change talks here, forcing leaders to spend time justifying the science behind global warming when they want to focus on ending it."[351]

A hacked server at the University of East Anglia's Climate Research Unit in the UK opened the door on the most full-blown scientific fraud since Lance Armstrong won his seventh Tour de France. Exposed by the hack were the emails exchanged among several high-profile climate scientists. Their willingness to suppress or modify data to better scale up the hysteria around global warming was unmistakable. Calling on Obama to boycott the talks over the "agenda-driven science" that Climategate exposed was none one other than Sarah Palin.[352] Her razzing alone should have prompted Obama to find the racial angle in the story and razz back, but that would have meant acknowledging the fraud.

On the climate front, Obama did no better at home than he did abroad. In his first term, with Democratic majorities in both Houses, he championed a Byzantine cap-and-trade bill known as the American Clean Energy and Security Act of 2009. In his memoir, he alludes to the bill but never by name. Nor are his readers allowed to see this sausage get made, or at least half-made.

Violating all his transparency promises, Obama's House allies failed to post the bill on line before plopping its fifteen hundred pages on the representatives' desks. After just three hours of debate, the bill passed but just barely. Hoping to be reelected, Democratic senators scrapped it in committee. Writes Obama, "If we hadn't yet passed climate change legislation…then it was directly attributable to the size of the mess we'd inherited, along with Republican obstruction and filibusters, all of which American voters could change by casting their ballots in November."[353] The voters apparently took Obama at his word that, under his plan, "electricity rates would necessarily skyrocket."[354] Come November, they sent sixty-three Democratic reps packing.

One failure that Obama did own up to was that of Solyndra, a heavily subsidized solar panel company that went spectacularly belly-up in 2011. As he would do with other conspicuous failures—Fast and Furious comes quickly to mind—Obama sloughed off some of the blame on to the

Bush administration, but here he is unusually candid about the ensuing embarrassment.

Obama writes, "Given the size of the default—not to mention the fact that my team had arranged for me to visit the company's California facility just as the first financial warning bells were beginning to ring—Solyndra became a PR nightmare." This much is true. A little more detail might have helped. During his visit, Obama boasted that Solyndra was one of the beneficiaries of his American Recovery and Reinvestment Act. The loan from US Energy Department came to a cool $536 million. Inspired by his own vision for a greener America, Obama made a comment that should be inscribed on his tomb, "The true engine of economic growth will always be companies like Solyndra."[355] Upon Solyndra's demise, Obama observed, "Republicans reveled."[356] I can attest to that. When I unexpectedly passed the plant on a California highway, I pulled off the road to take a picture to send to friends.

More interesting, as usual, are the stories that go untold, none more conspicuously lost to history than the exorcism of Van Jones. In a pre-dawn announcement on a Sunday morning, the White House announced that Jones, the so-called Green Energy Czar, was resigning. In his bitter resignation letter, Jones wrote, "On the eve of historic fights for health care and clean energy, opponents of reform have mounted a vicious smear campaign against me. They are using lies and distortions to distract and divide."

Actually, as *Politico* suggested, the charges leveled against Jones were accurate: he was a 9/11 "truther," a Marxist revolutionary in the not-so-distant past, and, worst of all from the Republicans' perspective, a guy not afraid to call them "assholes."[357] A champion of "intersectionality," the progressive buzzword of the moment, Jones was trying to fuse green issues with black ones. His forced exit gave Obama still another opportunity to beat the Tea Party over the head with the race cudgel. For whatever reason, Obama did not take it. Too bad. Including Jones's tale of woe would have injected some needed juice into the memoir.

Even larger than the Obamas' carbon footprint is their irony footprint. Wherever they go—Sidwell Friends, Copenhagen, Martha's

Vineyard—irony follows. Throughout the memoir, Obama makes no bones about his grudge against what he calls "Big Oil." He scolds BP at length for the disastrous oil spill in the Gulf of Mexico. He goes harder on the Koch brothers than he does on bin Laden. And yet, during a 2012 debate with Mitt Romney, he finds himself boasting, "So here's what I've done since I've been president. We have increased oil production to the highest levels in sixteen years."[358] One more note of unexamined irony: a "ferocious snowstorm" on the East Coast delayed Obama's return home from the Copenhagen global warming summit.

A Serious Mistake
Had Been Made

O n a structural level, the final pages of *A Promised Land* call to mind the climactic scene of *The Godfather*. While Obama busies himself with everyday White House affairs, his button men, like Michael Corleone's during his godson's baptism, were taking out his enemies. The sequence of events over a weeklong period in spring 2011 smells of orchestration.

The first on Obama's enemy's list was Donald Trump. What attracted Trump to the birther issue was not Obama's race, but his inexplicable resistance to sharing his birth certificate. As Philip Berg and Terry Lakin can attest, the resistance was fierce. If Obama were born in Hawaii on August 4, 1961, there would have been no reason to resist. I am not certain what Obama was hiding, but his behavior strongly suggests he was hiding something.

"Finally I decided I'd had enough,"[359] writes Obama. He called his *consigliore* Bob Bauer and told him "to go ahead and obtain the long-form birth certificate from its home in a bound volume, somewhere deep in the bowels of the Hawaii Vital Records office."[360] According to official White House documents, Obama's personal attorney, Judith Corley, sent a letter to Hawaii's Director of Health, Loretta Fuddy, on Friday, April 22, 2011. Using Perkins Coie stationery, Corley requested two copies of

Obama's original certificate of live birth and concluded the letter saying, "I will be coming to your offices to pick up the copies of the certificates." Obama sent an accompanying letter to verify the request.

On Monday, April 25, Fuddy sent Obama a letter granting his and Corley's request, saying, "Enclosed please find two certified copies of your original Certificate of Live Birth."[361] For whatever reason, perhaps for added drama, the White House felt compelled to create at least the impression that Corley had flown to Hawaii to retrieve the documents.

On the morning of Wednesday, April 27, Obama walked to the podium in the White House briefing room and shared the results of the Perkins Coie research. Still failing to appreciate how gingerly the media treated him, Obama writes, "I began by remarking on the fact that the national TV networks had all decided to break from their regularly scheduled programming to carry my remarks live—something they very rarely did." Yes, very rarely. The last comparable breakaway for a personal matter took place on July 25, 1969, when the networks gave Ted Kennedy fifteen minutes to assure America there was "no truth whatsoever" to any rumors of immoral conduct between him and the late Mary Jo Kopechne.

"Now, this issue has been going on for two, two and a half years now," Obama told the slice of the citizenry that watches TV in midmorning. "I think it started during the campaign. And I have to say that over the last two and a half years I have watched with bemusement, I've been puzzled at the degree to which this thing just kept on going." Obama knew when it started. He knew very well that Bauer and other Perkins Coie attorneys had been fighting off legal challenges since Philip Berg first filed suit in August 2008. At the briefing, he skipped those details. He did say, however, "We've had every official in Hawaii, Democrat and Republican, every news outlet that has investigated this, confirm that, yes, in fact, I was born in Hawaii, August 4, 1961, in Kapiolani Hospital."[362]

In his memoir, Obama quotes part of his statement. "We're not going to be able to do it if we are distracted," he writes of the serious work that lay ahead. "We're not going to be able to do it if we spend time vilifying each other. We're not going to be able to do it if we just make stuff up and pretend that facts are not facts. We're not going to be able to solve our problems if we get distracted by sideshows and carnival barkers."[363] Obama did not have to name the carnival barker. The media knew he meant Donald Trump. From his cellblock at the US Army Barracks at Fort Leavenworth, Lieutenant Colonel Lakin winced when Obama added, "We do not have time for this kind of silliness."

Obama was not finished with Trump. Immediately after the press briefing, he flew to Chicago to mock Trump some more on the Oprah show. While the president was going about his business the next two days—visiting tornado victims, speaking to schoolchildren, announcing the replacement of Defense Secretary Robert Gates with CIA Director Leon Panetta—his young gag writers Jon Favreau and Jon Lovett were busily working on his presentation for the upcoming White House Correspondents' Dinner. Donald Trump was to be in the audience. The *Washington Post* had invited Trump in much the spirit Michael Corleone would one day invite brother Fredo to go boating with him.

Obama's speechwriters were unaware that on April 29, the night before the Correspondents' Dinner, Obama had given the green light to whack Osama bin Laden. It would have been unseemly to tell jokes about a man who had no more than twenty-four hours left to live. So, he nixed the Osama jokes but kept the Trump ones.[364]

Obama appears to have lost more sleep over Trump than he did Osama. As he had to concede, Trump had managed to spin the release of the apparent birth certificate to his advantage. "Donald Trump had grudgingly acknowledged that he now believed I was born in Hawaii," Obama writes, "while taking full credit for having forced me—on behalf of the American people—to certify my status."[365] Trump's effrontery could not stand. It was time for revenge. Here is what Obama dished out at the dinner, much of which is excerpted in the memoir:

> Donald Trump is here tonight! (Laughter and applause.) Now, I know that he's taken some flak lately, but no one is happier, no one is prouder to put this birth certificate matter to rest than the Donald. (Laughter.) And that's because he can finally get back to focusing on the

issues that matter—like, did we fake the moon landing? What really happened in Roswell? And where are Biggie and Tupac?

But all kidding aside, obviously, we all know about your credentials and breadth of experience. (Laughter.) For example—no, seriously, just recently, in an episode of Celebrity Apprentice—(laughter)—at the steakhouse, the men's cooking team cooking did not impress the judges from Omaha Steaks. And there was a lot of blame to go around. But you, Mr. Trump, recognized that the real problem was a lack of leadership. And so ultimately, you didn't blame Lil' Jon or Meatloaf. (Laughter.) You fired Gary Busey. (Laughter.) And these are the kind of decisions that would keep me up at night. (Laughter and applause.) Well handled, sir. (Laughter.) Well handled.

> Say what you will about Mr. Trump, he certainly would bring some change to the White House. Let's see what we've got up there. (Laughter.) (Screens show "Trump White House Resort and Casino.")[366]

"The audience howled as Trump sat in silence, cracking a tepid smile," writes Obama. "I couldn't begin to guess what went through his mind during the few minutes I spent publicly ribbing him."[367] CIA Director Leon Panetta, who sat with Obama that evening, adds, "The audience, save Trump, reeled in laughter, none aware of the historic drama unfolding beneath Obama's remarks."[368] None was aware, that is, save for Obama and Panetta.

Although the media would go on to speculate that Trump's "humiliation" at the 2011 dinner prompted him to seek revenge by running for president, one surprisingly honest *Washington Post* reporter thought otherwise. Roxanne Roberts was sitting next to Trump. "With cameras aimed at him, Trump smiled at Obama's jokes and waved at the crowd," wrote Roberts. When she contacted Trump about the dinner in 2016, he breezily dismissed the speculation that he had been humiliated. "It's such a false narrative," Trump told her. "I had a phenomenal time. I had a great evening." Roberts believed him.[369]

Coke/Obama had made the amateurish marketing blunder of accepting the Pepsi/Trump Challenge. Obama would live to regret it. Starting in 2015, Trump had a six-year run to say whatever he liked about Obama, and those comments have not left Obama smiling, not even tepidly. "What I knew was that he was a spectacle," writes a still seething Obama, "and in the United States of America in 2011, that was a form of power. Trump trafficked in a currency that, however shallow, seemed to gain more purchase with each passing day."[370] By the time Obama's memoir was published, the carnival barker had delivered four years of peace and prosperity, a reality Obama and his media allies will never admit.

On the day after the dinner, April 30, at about 1:30 p.m. eastern time, Obama gave his final approval for the attack on the bin Laden compound. A half hour later, two Black Hawk helicopters carrying twenty-three SEAL team members took off from Jalalabad Airfield in Afghanistan and launched Operation Neptune Spear into the history books.

Obama notes, "This was the first and only time as president that I'd watch a military operation unfold in real time." [371] That said, he shares no specifics. What happened in those twenty minutes, especially after the SEAL team entered the house, Obama chooses not to discuss, not even in retrospect. The details were not pretty, nor do they align with the information Obama and his people supplied the media in the immediate wake of the assault. Obama also refrains from serving up any snippets from his speech on the night of May 1 announcing Osama's death. Crafted by adviser Ben Rhodes, the speech would later become a source of controversy, not just for its inaccuracies, but also for the very fact that Obama gave it.

The following afternoon, May 2, future CIA director John Brennan met with the press to clarify details. By profession and personal inclination, he had no particular interest in telling the truth. Even more obviously than Obama, he was spinning events to bolster Obama's electoral chances in 2012. "The concern was that bin Laden would oppose any type of capture operation," Brennan told the press. "Indeed, he did. It was a firefight. He, therefore, was killed in that firefight and that's when the remains were removed." As would be revealed within days, there was no plan to capture Osama. He did not resist. There was no firefight. Equally false was Brennan's overarching message, namely that Obama "made what I believe was one of the gutsiest calls of any president in recent memory."[372]

What follows is the somewhat more accurate account offered by the CIA's Panetta in his 2014 book, *Worthy Fights*. Panetta monitored the action from CIA headquarters in Langley, Virginia:

> Between the second and third floors, a bearded young man whom the assaulters recognized as Khalid bin Laden, bin Laden's son, was shot and killed. As the SEALs moved to the third floor, a tall, bearded man poked his head out of a doorway. A member of our team, recognizing him instantly, shot at him and missed.
>
> The man disappeared back into the room, and an AK-47 was visible in the doorjamb. Team members moved towards the door.
>
> As they moved inside the room, two young girls and an adult woman rushed the SEALs. Our operator grabbed the girls and shoved them to the side as they screamed in fear. One woman shouted at the man upstairs, calling him "sheikh."
>
> Our team members saw the bearded man and shot him twice, once above the left eye and once in the chest. A woman in the room, whom we later learned was bin Laden's third wife, was shot in the leg, but not seriously wounded.[373]

Obama's baptism scene had one final act. Also on May 2, "wingman" Eric Holder met with Obama at the White House with no reason given on the logs. The two men had much to discuss. The following day Holder had an all-day oversight review scheduled with the House Judiciary Committee. Holder would be pleased to discuss the hit on bin Laden. Holder, however, was not so keen to talk about an operation called "Fast and Furious."

As to background, in the early morning hours of December 15, 2010, Border Patrol Agent Brian Terry became the first known American victim of this inexplicable program. Run through the Bureau of Alcohol, Tobacco, and Firearms (ATF) and under the auspices of the DOJ, Fast and Furious defies explanation. To this day, no one in an official capacity has ever offered a credible rationale for its existence.

Most likely, the White House thought that if American-purchased guns were allowed free flow across the border, a steady stream of news about Mexican mass killings with American weapons might persuade the American public to support a crackdown on guns. No other explanation makes sense. Terry's death forced this covert program into the open. Obama's response from the beginning was to plead ignorance, and Holder's was to lie and conceal.

In February 2011, the Department of Justice denied there was any such program. A month later, Obama admitted to Mexican journalist Jorge Ramos that "a serious mistake may have been made." Although insisting that neither he nor Holder had anything to do with Fast and Furious, Obama noted that Holder had assigned an inspector general to investigate. "And you were not even informed about it?" asked an incredulous Ramos. "Absolutely not," said Obama.[374]

Once dragged into the limelight, Holder did nothing but stonewall. During the hearing on May 3, Republican Darrell Issa asked Holder when he first learned about the program. Said Holder, "I probably heard about Fast and Furious for the first time over the last few weeks." Republican Jason Chaffetz caught the inconsistency. He noted that six weeks prior, on March 22, Obama had told Ramos that Holder had already launched an investigation. "How did it *not* come to your attention?" Chaffetz asked.

Holder had no good answer. He claimed the DOJ's inspector general was looking into the program as though that were attention enough. He also showed no particular interest in responding to a House subpoena in anything resembling good faith. Bristling throughout the interview, Holder found it "offensive" that Issa would think anyone at the DOJ was responsible for Terry's death. "I have felt their pain," he said of the nation's law enforcement officers.[375] Needless to say, in the wake of the bin Laden assault, Holder's testimony on Fast and Furious scarcely made the news. In *A Promised Land*, Obama makes no mention whatsoever of the program or the death of Brian Terry.

It does not to take much in the way of imagination to think Obama's people orchestrated this weeklong sequence of events. Of the four key dates in this sequence only two were fixed in advance: the April 30 Correspondents' Dinner and the May 2 congressional hearing. Obama could have revealed the birth certificate at any time, and he had a broad window of opportunity to order the Osama hit and an even broader window to announce it. It seems *likely* that his people timed the birth certificate drop to humble Trump at the Correspondents' Dinner and *possible* that they timed the Osama action and especially the hasty announcement of its success to push both the birth certificate and Holder's congressional testimony off the front pages.

A May 2015 article by veteran journalist Seymour Hersh suggests there was no urgency as to when the assault on the Abbottabad compound took place. Among other accomplishments, Hersh broke the story of 1968's My Lai massacre and of American prisoner abuse in Iraq's Abu Ghraib prison in 2004. In his carefully researched, well-sourced, ten-thousand-word piece in the *London Review of Books* Hersh offers what is likely the most accurate account to date of the killing of Osama.[376] To be sure, Hersh has his critics, but Carlotta Gall, who spent twelve years covering Pakistan and Afghanistan for the *New York Times*, is not one of them. As Gall observes, "From the moment it was announced to the public, the tale of how Osama bin Laden met his death in a Pakistani hill town in May 2011 has been a changeable feast."[377]

According to Hersh, "the most blatant lie" Obama and his staff told was that the senior generals of Pakistan's army and Inter-Services Intelligence agency (ISI) were unaware of the planned raid. Another noteworthy White House lie was that the CIA learned of bin Laden's location by relentlessly tracking his couriers. According to Hersh, a former senior Pakistani intelligence officer betrayed the secret in return for some chunk of the twenty-five-million-dollar reward offered by the United States.

Hersh makes a convincing argument that, in fact, the ISI had captured Osama in Afghanistan in 2006 and held him as hostage to keep al-Qaeda in check. As in *The Godfather's* hospital scene, the guards slipped away—in this case, at the sound of the helicopter rotors—to allow the assault to unfold without resistance. Unfortunately for Osama, he had no son like Michael shrewd enough to sense the danger and spirit the ailing old man out of harm's way.

"Of course the guys knew the target was bin Laden and he was there under Pakistani control," a retired official American official told Hersh. "Otherwise, they would not have done the mission without air cover. It was clearly and absolutely a premeditated murder." "Murder" is a little strong—after all, war is hell—but had a police SWAT team executed a similar raid in the United States and killed an unarmed person of color, Obama would be the first to condemn the cops, even if he didn't have all the facts.

As Hersh's sources explained, Pakistan officials would not have allowed the American helicopters to enter their air space were there not a quid pro quo. The "quo" included eighteen new F-16 fighter aircraft and covert cash payments to senior Pakistani officials. Exiting the compound was potentially much hairier than entering as one of the helicopters was damaged upon landing and subsequently blown up by the SEALs. That explosion had to attract attention at nearby Pakistani military installations. Instead of scurrying out on the one viable chopper, the remaining SEALs waited for the backup to arrive. Said the official, "They would not have blown the chopper—no commo [communication] gear is worth a dozen lives—unless they knew they were safe."

To take the pressure off the cooperating Pakistanis, the White House was supposed to wait a week and then announce that Osama had been killed by a drone strike in Afghanistan. The blown helicopter gave Obama and his political people the excuse to press for an immediate announcement. This "outraged" Defense Secretary Robert Gates. "That we killed him, I said, is all we needed to say," writes Gates in his memoir *Duty*. "Everybody in that room agreed to keep mum on details. That commitment lasted about five hours. The initial leaks came from the White House and CIA. They just couldn't wait to brag and to claim credit."[378]

Panetta attributed the decision to go public to Obama. After reviewing the details, writes Panetta, "the President was now convinced. 'We shoot for tonight,' he said, regarding the plan for announcing the action. 'Let's have a draft within an hour.'"[379]

This political grandstanding exposed the role of the Pakistani officials. "They felt Obama sold them down the river," Hersh's source told him. "We've had a four-year lapse in co-operation. It's taken that long for the Pakistanis to trust us again in the military-to-military counterterrorism relationship." Again, these details will have to wait for Volume II—as if.

Volume I ends in melodramatic triumph: "I had to decide whether or not to authorize a raid deep inside Pakistan to go after a target we believed to be Osama bin Laden—and whatever else happened, I was likely to end up a one-term president if I got it wrong." Depending on who told him what, Obama may have even believed that. Equally possible is that he knew the risk was minimal, and if the raid were well timed—say, the day after his takedown of Donald Trump and the day before Holder's House testimony—Trump would be toxic, and he, Obama, would be untouchable.

What follows the Osama saga in *A Promised Land*, as the reader might expect, is page after page of self-congratulatory prose tempered by Obama's well-rehearsed faux modesty. In those many pages, one sentence stands out: "For all the pride and satisfaction I took in the success of our mission in Abbottabad, the truth was that I hadn't felt the same exuberance as I had on the night the healthcare bill passed."[380] Strange as it seems, I suspect Obama here is telling the truth.

One final postscript, as reported in *Politico* on June 28, 2012, "The House has voted to hold Attorney General Eric Holder in contempt of Congress over his failure to turn over documents related to the Fast and Furious scandal, the first time Congress has taken such a dramatic move against a sitting Cabinet official."[381] Seventeen Democrats signed on to the resolution. Only sixty-seven Democrats voted against it. The vote to hold the attorney general in contempt was arguably the purest bipartisan moment in Obama's misbegotten first term since the vote to defund ACORN.

A month after the dust settled, Bauer returned to private practice so he could once again represent the Obama campaign and the DNC. Said Obama of Bauer at the time, "He has exceptional judgment, wisdom, and intellect, and he will continue to be one of my close advisers." Bauer would offer that advice from the plush offices of the firm to which he returned, Perkins Coie.

In April 2016, when the DNC learned that its computers had been hacked, its staff alerted Perkins Coie, and the firm, in turn, recommended a private cybersecurity outfit called CrowdStrike to clean up the mess. No need to bring in the FBI. That same memorable year, 2016, Perkins Coie retained Fusion GPS to create the infamous Steele dossier. I would suggest that a firm capable of commissioning the Steele dossier would have no trouble dummying up a birth certificate. Just sayin'.

Trump may have moved on from the birther issue, but neither Bauer nor Obama did. In March 2019, Bauer used the pretext of former Trump attorney Michael Cohen's House committee testimony to assault Trump anew in the pages of the *Atlantic*.[382] "Trump repeatedly hawked the lies that Obama was born in Kenya," wrote Bauer.

This was false. Trump did question the mystery surrounding Obama's origins, but despite their digging, the media could find no instance in which he claimed Obama was born in Kenya. As Breitbart reported, it was the young Obama who claimed Kenyan birth when first positioning himself in the literary marketplace.

BARACK OBAMA'S PROMISED LAND

No fewer than a dozen times in the course of this article did Bauer use the words "race," "racist," or "racism" to attack Trump. The article was well timed. A month later, Joe Biden would announce his candidacy for the presidency claiming that Trump's racism motivated him to run. Biden centered his racism charge on Trump's reaction to a 2017 incident in Charlottesville, shamelessly misrepresenting Trump's comments about the violent clash. "We are in the battle for the soul of this nation," said Biden. He warned that if Trump were reelected, "He will forever and fundamentally alter the character of this nation, who we are, and I cannot stand by and watch that happen."[383] Bauer could not stand by either. He and his wife, Anita Dunn, played major roles in Biden's campaign. In fact, Dunn ran it.

Journalists Threatened, Arrested, Beaten, Attacked

Also on Obama's hit list in late April 2011 were some of the very people laughing at his jokes at the Correspondent's Dinner. Obama's Department of Justice had been tracking one of the attendees for at least a year. That would be James Rosen, the chief Washington correspondent for Fox News. Rosen's affiliation with Fox likely put a bull's-eye on his back. CBS reporter Sharyl Attkisson, who broke the Fast and Furious story, had been enduring electronic harassment for months. Other journalists, many of them with the Associated Press, would soon be targeted. That Saturday night, however, the correspondents were encouraged to think Obama was their champion.

"You know, in the last months, we've seen journalists threatened, arrested, beaten, attacked, and in some cases even killed simply for doing their best to bring us the story, to give people a voice, and to hold leaders accountable," Obama told the jovial crowd. "And through it all, we've seen daring men and women risk their lives for the simple idea that no one should be silenced, and everyone deserves to know the truth. That's what you do. At your best that's what journalism is."[384]

Obama does not recount this part of the speech in his memoir. It might have reminded these "daring men and women" that although they had his back, he did not have theirs.

The joke, as it turned out, was on them. They would not realize how unfunny the joke was until the media broke the news in May 2013. As reported by the *Washington Post*—the same outfit that invited Trump—the DOJ had been monitoring the comings and goings of James Rosen since 2010. What most troubled the *Post* and other media about the DOJ was the use of search warrants to investigate a reporter and the threat to prosecute him under the terms of Espionage Act as an "as an aider, abettor and/or co-conspirator."

Rosen was not the only one who had been tracked. The previous week the *Post* reported that federal investigators had obtained records covering two months of more than twenty telephone lines assigned to the Associated Press. "Search warrants like these have a severe chilling effect on the free flow of important information to the public," First Amendment lawyer Charles Tobin told the *Post*. "That's a very dangerous road to go down."[385]

Sharyl Attkisson is uncertain as to when exactly certain forces began to cyber-gaslight her, but it was well before the Correspondents' Dinner. A WikiLeaks document purloined from the global intelligence firm Stratfor in 2010 claimed that Obama's all-purpose fixer John Brennan was "behind the witch hunts of investigative journalists learning information from inside the beltway sources."[386]

Some months after the Correspondents' Dinner, the White House initiated an "Internal Threat Program." In hunting down leakers in departments as benign as education and agriculture, White House operatives went even further astray than Nixon's "plumbers," who, for all their notoriety, stuck to national security. In a move that the Stasi might admire, the Obama administration made everyone a plumber. The program's strategic plan actually mandated that supervisors "penalize clearly identifiable failures to report security infractions and violations, including any lack of self-reporting."[387] In a *New York Times* op-ed, liberal First Amendment lawyer James Goodale said out loud what others were thinking: "President Obama will surely pass President Richard Nixon as the worst president ever on issues of national security and press freedom."[388]

In *A Promised Land*, Obama does talk about the suppression of journalists but only in other countries. In the hated Russia, he writes, "Independent journalists and civic leaders found themselves monitored by the FSB (the modern incarnation of the KGB)—or, in some cases, turned up dead."[389] And then in Egypt, Obama tells us, "The State Department worked diligently behind the scenes to protect journalists, free political dissidents, and widen the space for civic engagement."[390] But American journalists enjoyed no such support, especially those like Rosen and Attkisson whose reporting threatened the powerful.

If American journalists chose to forget Obama's paranoid crackdown on free speech, the reviewer from UK's leftist *Guardian* did not. "The prosecution of twice as many whistleblowers as all his predecessors combined is not mentioned," lamented Gary Younge in his review of *A Promised Land*. "Liberals struggle to subject Obama to the rigorous critique that the power he held demands. They are always liable to give him the benefit of the doubt, as if his position didn't grant him enough benefits already."

Younge, who is himself black, is a professor at the University of Manchester. He adds a quirky aside about a course he taught on how the media treated Obama. "I stopped teaching it in the next semester," he wrote, "because the students were simply unwilling, or unable, to criticise him."[391] By 2016, alarmed by Trump's emergence, the *Washington Post* and *New York Times* proved unwilling or unable to criticize Obama's use of state power to subvert Trump's presidency, but that, I guess, is a story for *A Promised Land II*.

The Sound of Car Locks Clicking

Soon after Eric Holder was confirmed as attorney general in 2009 he gave a speech to his new employees in honor of Black History Month. It proved memorable. "Though this nation has proudly thought of itself as an ethnic melting pot," said Holder, "in things racial we have always been and continue to be, in too many ways, essentially a nation of cowards." The "cowards" line got people's attention. It was "a true enough observation but not necessarily the headline we were looking for at the end of my first few weeks in office," writes Obama.[392]

It is true that white Americans are reluctant to speak about race, but Obama prefers not to say why. Like Holder, he refuses to acknowledge the soft-core terror he and his fellow progressives have imposed upon the land. In July 2009, friend and Harvard professor Louis Henry Gates gave Obama an opportunity to ease people's fears. Returning to his home after a trip to China, the keyless Gates and his driver had to force the back door open to gain entry. Trying to be a good neighbor, a woman called Cambridge Police to report a potential break-in.

When Officer James Crowley arrived at the scene, he explained he was investigating a report of a break-in in progress. Gates shot back, "Why, because I am a black man in America?" When Crowley asked Gates to speak with him outside, Gates shot back, "I'll speak with your mama outside." Crowley warned Gates several times he would be arrested if he kept up what the police report calls his "tumultuous behavior." Gates kept at it and was arrested for disorderly conduct.[393]

In explaining why he and other African Americans instinctively sided with Gates, Obama once again "darkens the canvas," this time by doing a "quick inventory" of his own grievances. In *A Promised Land* he talks of "unmerited traffic stops," of being followed by store security, and of hearing "the sound of car locks clicking as I walked across a street, dressed in a suit and tie, in the middle of the day."[394] I'll buy the unmerited stops. Just about every time the police have pulled me over it was unmerited. At least I thought so. As to the clicking car locks, with that claim Obama imagined a Chicago very nearly as fantastic as Jussie Smollett's.

Even if all these charges were true, Obama knows why people might just look upon young black men suspiciously. He admitted as much in his Father's Day speech in Chicago. In a rare honest moment, even Jesse Jackson acknowledged the conundrum. "There is nothing more painful to me at this stage in my life," said Jackson in a 1993 Operation PUSH meeting in Chicago, "than to walk down the street and hear footsteps and start thinking about robbery, then look around and see someone white and feel relieved."[395]

If Obama were unaware of the excessive crime rates among African Americans, he could be forgiven, but he does know. In 2009, after the Gates arrest, he blew his opportunity to speak honestly to the issue.

"I don't know, not having been there and not seeing all the facts, what role race played in that," he said when questioned by a reporter. "But I think it's fair to say, number one, any of us would be pretty angry; number two, that the Cambridge police acted stupidly in arresting somebody when there was already proof that they were in their own home; and number three, what I think we know separate and apart from this incident is that there is a long history in this country of African Americans and Latinos being stopped by law enforcement disproportionately."

In *A Promised Land,* Obama claims to have been surprised by the reporter's question. A skeptic might think otherwise. The answer sounds too rehearsed, but in either case, the reaction to the "acted stupidly" remark, especially by the police, caught Obama and his aides by surprise. As it turns out, Crowley was a model cop and Obama supporter who ran the department's racial sensitivity training. He refused to apologize, and his police commissioner backed him. When Obama's communications guy, Robert Gibbs, asked Obama if he wanted to offer a clarification of his remarks, Obama responded, or so he tells us in his memoir, "What am I clarifying? I thought I was pretty clear the first time."[396]

Eventually Obama agreed to a "damage-control plan." That plan took the form of the infamous "beer summit" with Gates, Crowley, and blue-collar Joe Biden thrown in for race and, yes, class balance. Obama suggests that he agreed to the summit not because he said anything wrong but because what he did say was polling badly.

The Gates incident took place just months into the new presidency. Already Obama insinuated that his self-sacrificing white grandmother and a standout white cop were racists or something very much like it, in both cases on the flimsiest of evidence. In so doing, Obama helped ensure that white people who valued their livelihoods, especially those in government, would remain as cowardly as Holder thought them to be.

"Cant was the only way a sensibly self-protective person would talk about race in public—and when it came to civil rights, every place was public," writes Christopher Caldwell in his well-observed 2019 book, *The Age of Entitlement*. If every place was public, no place was more public than Obama's Washington. One can only imagine the anxiety felt by a person of non-color knowing that an "imperfectly calibrated phrase" could end his or her career in a heartbeat.

Reflecting on his reaction to the Gates arrest, Obama absolves himself and projects the blame onto white America. "We'd grown skilled at suppressing our reactions to minor slights," writes Obama—the "we" being he and other African Americans in his elite circle—"ever ready to give white colleagues the benefit of the doubt, remaining mindful that all but the most careful discussions of race risked triggering in them a mild panic."[397] What they had grown skilled at was not so much suppressing slights but interpreting all slights as racially motivated. Whether intentionally or not, Obama had helped usher in the age of the *microaggression*.

Eating Chicken and Listening to Stevie Wonder

In 1965, Daniel Patrick Moynihan, then an undersecretary of labor, had yet to learn that truth was about as welcome in Lyndon Johnson's Washington as a White House aide with a YMCA problem. In his provocative report, *The Negro Family: The Case for National Action*, Moynihan argued that starting in about 1962 unemployment rates for black men, which had historically tracked with white unemployment rates, began to diverge downwards. As a corollary, welfare cases, which had historically declined as employment increased, were now increasing despite growth in employment. The federal government, Moynihan suggested, was rewarding fatherlessness. That had to change.

"In a word, a national effort towards the problems of Negro Americans must be directed towards the question of family structure," wrote Moynihan. "The object should be to strengthen the Negro family so as to enable it to raise and support its members as do other families." Had Moynihan stopped there, he might not have caught so much heat, but he argued against additional federal intervention. "After that," he wrote, "how this group of Americans chooses to run its affairs, take advantage of its opportunities, or fail to do so, is none of the nation's business."[398] In recommending autonomy for the black community, however, he was denying "civil rights" leaders their leverage with the federal government. Many of them shared their discontent with the president.

Ignoring Moynihan's conclusions, Johnson and his successors made it the nation's business to appease those leaders. The results were catastrophic. In the forty-three years between the report's publication and Obama's Father's Day speech in Chicago, out-of-wedlock births in the black community had increased from 25 percent to 65 percent. As progressive orthodoxy on race grew harder to defend, progressives grew less tolerant of dissent. Holder and Obama had to be aware of the chokehold their allies had on speech in public forums, but it was only that chokehold that kept the race industry alive.

If anything, it was Holder's race that protected his career and enabled his confirmation as attorney general. As with Obama, his ancestors did nothing to afford him that protection. They came to the U.S. voluntarily in the twentieth century, his father, like his maternal grandparents, from Barbados. Like generations of immigrants before them, they came looking for freedom and opportunity and found both long before anyone even heard the phrase "racial equity."

"If we are to make progress in this area," Holder told the DOJ staffers, "we must feel comfortable enough with one another and tolerant enough of each other to have frank conversations about the racial matters that continue to divide us."[399] In the *City Journal*, attorney and scholar Heather Mac Donald broke down Holder's "frank" into its component parts, all subsets of a half-century-long progressive disinformation campaign: "Police stop and arrest blacks at disproportionate rates because of racism; blacks are disproportionately in prison because of racism; blacks are failing in school because of racist inequities in school funding; the black poverty rate is the highest in the country because of racism; blacks were given mortgages that they couldn't afford because of racism."

As Obama did on Father's Day in 2008, Mac Donald detailed how family breakdown has led almost inexorably to the host of pathologies that plague black America. "The issue of race in the United States is more complex than polite company is usually allowed to express," she concluded. "If Eric Holder wants to crank up our racial preoccupations even further, let him at least do so with a full airing of the facts."[400]

Excluding Father's Day 2008, Obama has refused to air the facts that would lead to an honest discussion of race. No one is quite sure who has been enforcing Obama's silence, but the most cited suspect goes unmentioned in *A Promised Land*. That would be international man of mystery, George Soros. Soros *is*, in fact, what progressives accuse the Koch brothers of being: a hugely powerful and omnipresent mover and shaker. Reportedly, Obama met with the billionaire financier in his New York offices in December 2006.

Until that meeting, Soros favored Hillary Clinton's candidacy. It would appear that Obama got Soros's blessing. A few weeks later, when Obama announced that he was forming an exploratory committee, Soros sent him a check for the maximum personal donation within hours.[401] No doubt, Soros's massive contributions through a wide range of leftist organizations helped shape Obama's presidency, but there is little evidence of direct, hands-on guidance.

For other, less obvious candidates, however, there is ample evidence. No single one of these candidates controlled Obama's presidency, nor did they coordinate their efforts. Indeed, they occasionally fought among themselves. Working individually for the most part, they succeeded in defining Obama's presidency for the simple reason that they were all pulling Obama in the same direction.

Within three weeks of his memorable speech on Father's Day 2008, one of them pulled hard. That would be Chicago's then-most prominent baby daddy, Jesse Jackson. Jackson was "overheard" talking to another black guest on a hot mic at the Fox News studio. The cynic suspects that Jackson wanted his message to be heard, and he knew that at Fox someone would think to leak it. If so, he got his way.

Jackson said (excuse my French), "See, Barack been, um, talking down to black people on this faith-based—I wanna cut his nuts out." Here Jackson made a sharp slicing motion with his hands and continued, "Barack—he's talking down to black people—telling niggers how to behave."[402] Jackson later apologized but without even feigning sincerity. Obama seems to have gotten the message. From that day forward, Jackson's weary, self-destructive progressivism carried the day as it had since he assumed leadership of the flailing civil rights movement forty years prior.

Obama does not talk about Jackson's comments in *A Promised Land*. That's a shame. Team Obama's behind-the-scenes response to the Jackson threat might have enticed even a Republican or two to buy the book. What seems clear, though, is that Jesse Jackson's very authenticity scared Obama. When Jackson ran for president in 1988, no one questioned *his* birthplace or his roots or his eligibility.

This evidence for the second likely candidate surfaced in December 2014 following the lethal ambush of two police officers in Brooklyn. Former New York City Mayor Rudy Giuliani attributed some of the blame to Obama. In explaining his rationale, Giuliani said, "He has had Al Sharpton to the White House 80, 85 times. You make Al Sharpton a close adviser, you are going to turn the police in America against you."[403]

Hoping to catch Giuliani in a lie, the *Washington Post* commissioned a fact-checker to set the record straight. Giuliani did not back down: "We're talking about a man with a record that is astoundingly outrageous, a man who was a tax cheat, a liar…who has made allegations against police officers constantly." When asked whether he thought Sharpton was a legitimate civil rights activist, Giuliani shot back, "Are you out of your mind? Are you living on Mars?"

The *Post* did an exhaustive follow-up on Giuliani's claim. The fact-checker acknowledged that Sharpton had emerged as "an unexpected ally of the White House on race relations" and was considered "Obama's go-to man on race." As to the number of times Sharpton went to the White House during the first five years of Obama's presidency, the fact-checker had to concede, "There were at least 72 instances since Obama took office where Sharpton visited the White House for official business."[404]

A 2003 article by Jake Tapper in *Salon*, when Sharpton was threatening a presidential run, highlighted some of the baggage Sharpton had to lug with him: his lead role in the infamous Tawana Brawley hoax; his anti-white protest at Freddy's Fashion Mart in Harlem that turned deadly; his rallying cry during the lethal Crown Heights pogrom, "If Jews want to get it on, tell them to pin their yarmulkes back and come over to my house"; and, perhaps most problematic in the age of intersectional bliss, his trashing of "Socrates and them Greek homos."[405] Then, as Giuliani also noted, there were the millions of dollars in unpaid taxes.

Those interested in how the clownish Sharpton sloughed off his Byzantine history and finessed his way past Jesse Jackson to become Obama's "go-to man on race" will not find the answer in *A Promised Land*. Here is all that Obama has to say about Sharpton: "Meanwhile, there were activists and intellectuals who supported me but viewed my campaign in purely symbolic terms, akin to earlier races mounted by Shirley Chisholm, Jesse Jackson, and Al Sharpton, a useful if transitory platform from which to raise a prophetic voice against racial injustice."[406] That's the sum of it, one single mention, not a word about those seventy-two *official* visits.

Sharpton had little inherent power and less money, but as the contemporary avatar of a powerful moral legacy, he did not need either. Serving as the conduit through which old school black America voiced its concerns, he had influence, and that's what counted most. That voice frightened Obama. At least since his failed 2000 bid for Congress, if not before, Obama knew that African Americans with genuine roots thought him an impostor.

"Almost from the start, the race was a disaster," he writes of his campaign to unseat incumbent Bobby Rush, a former Black Panther. "A few weeks in, the rumblings from the Rush camp began: *Obama's an outsider; he's backed by white folks; he's a Harvard elitist. And that name—is he even Black?*"[407]

Rush and his other black opponent in the 2000 race sensed the same vulnerability that Jesse Jackson would exploit in 2008 and that Sharpton would exploit for the eight years after that, namely Obama's felt lack of authenticity as a black man. "He went to Harvard and became an educated fool," said Rush during the 2000 campaign. "Barack is a person who read about the civil-rights protests and thinks he knows all about it." Fellow State Senator Donne Trotter rode him harder still. "Barack is viewed in part to be the white man in blackface in our community," said Trotter. "You have only to look at his supporters. Who pushed him to get where he is so fast? It's these individuals in Hyde Park, who don't always have the best interest of the community in mind."[408] In *Becoming*, Michelle sums up what Rush and Trotter were saying: "He's not one of us, in other words. Barack wasn't a real black man, like them...."[409]

As hard as he tries, Obama fails to convince anyone that he is just another black guy. When, in *A Promised Land*, he imagines himself as one of "four longtime friends, African Americans from the South Side of Chicago, eating chicken and listening to Stevie Wonder,"[410] informed readers have to feel a little bit sorry for him. They know Obama grew up not in the South Side of Chicago but on the South Shore of Oahu with his white mother and grandparents. More aware readers remember Obama as the biracial metrosexual who, according to college friend Phil Boerner, "enjoyed exploring museums such as the Guggenheim, the Met and the American Museum of Natural History and browsing in bookstores such as the Strand and the Barnes & Noble opposite Columbia."[411]

For all their many flaws, Jesse Jackson and Al Sharpton never had to exploit their wives and children to claim their place as descendants of slaves and victims of slavery's aftereffects. Obama did, and he did so often enough to establish wife Michelle as the third and perhaps most important member of this time-defying triumvirate. Together, they kept Obama locked in a past that left him feeling guilty for never having lived it.

Michelle never lived that past either. In *Becoming* she writes that Barack pictured her family as "a black version of Leave It to Beaver."[412] For all her good fortune, however, she continued to relish playing victim. A classic case involved her incognito trip to a Virginia Target store in September 2011. On the David Letterman show in March 2012, a cheerful Michelle shared her tale. "I have to tell you something about this trip though," she said with a smile. "No one knew that was me. Because a woman actually walked up to me, right? I was in the detergent aisle, and she said—I kid you not—she said, 'Excuse me, I just have to ask you something,' and I thought, 'Cover's blown.' She said, 'Can you reach on that shelf and hand me the detergent?'" She laughed, explaining that the woman was short and needed help from Michelle, who is nearly six-feet tall. "That was my interaction. I felt so good," said Michelle. When Letterman asked whether the woman recognized the First Lady, Michelle answered, "She had no idea who I was."[413]

In December 2014, four months after the shooting of Michael Brown in Ferguson, Missouri, *People* magazine interviewed the Obamas for a story focusing on their encounters with racism. Michelle began by saying, "I tell this story—I mean, even as the First Lady." Here, she suggests that the tale has already become folklore. Michelle continued, "During that wonderfully publicized trip I took to Target, not highly disguised, the only person who came up to me in the store was a woman who asked me to help her take something off a shelf. Because she didn't see me as the First Lady, she saw me as someone who could help her."

On Letterman, Michelle did not impute any particular race to the woman in question, nor did she suggest any motive other than the woman's inability to reach the top shelf.

Here, Michelle wants the readers of *People* to believe that the woman was white, that she recognized the "not highly disguised" Michelle, and treated her like *the help* even knowing she was the First Lady. Michelle did not want this to be seen as an isolated incident. She concluded, "Those kinds of things happen in life. So it isn't anything new."[414] Michelle was not the first person of color to conjure a slight out of thin air, but for her to spread this pernicious fable as First Lady did nothing but reinforce white guilt and black anxiety. "Imagine," readers were primed to think, "even the First Lady!"

Although Obama knows better, he presents Michelle's insecurities and resentments as indisputable truths. In *A Promised Land*, for instance, he cites the time that Michelle said unthinkingly, "For the first time in my adult lifetime, I'm really proud of my country." She made this much too telling remark during the 2008 campaign upon seeing the enthusiasm among white people for Obama's candidacy.

Obama admits Michelle made a "textbook gaffe." As he knows, a candidate's wife is expected to be proud of her country under normal circumstances, but he cannot leave it at that. As in the Philadelphia speech, he feels compelled to gird himself with the Kevlar of his wife's cultural heritage.

"I understood this to be part of a larger and uglier agenda out there," Obama writes of the negative reaction to Michelle's comment, "a slowly accruing, deliberately negative portrait of us built from stereotypes, stoked by fear, and meant to feed a general nervousness about the idea of a Black person making the country's most important decisions with his Black family in the White House."[415] The critical word here is "us."

I am not sure if Obama understands just how insulting is his repeated effort to wrap himself in the *us* and demonize the *them*. For Obama, the Tea Party serves the same function as Hillary's "basket of deplorables," the Trump supporters Hillary laughingly described as "racist, sexist, homophobic, xenophobic, Islamaphobic—you name it."[416] Among the more delusional passages from *A Promised Land* is the following:

> One night toward the end of our road trip, after we'd tucked the girls in, Michelle caught a glimpse of a Tea Party rally on TV—with its enraged flag-waving and inflammatory slogans. She seized the remote and turned off the set, her expression hovering somewhere between rage and resignation.
>
> "It's a trip, isn't it?" she said.
>
> "What is?"
>
> "That they're scared of you. Scared of us."
>
> She shook her head and headed for bed.[417]

There is that *us* again, but those flag-wavers were not the ones scared of *us*. Obama was. In a May 2011 interview activist professor Cornel West nailed Obama on this fear. "All he has known culturally is white," said West. "He is just as human as I am, but that is his cultural formation. When he meets an independent black brother, it is frightening."[418]

Obama tried much too hard to gain the acceptance of the authentic *us,* those African Americans whose traditions were forged in slavery, most proximate among them, wife Michelle. Although Obama seems a natural as a father, his overly affectionate embrace of Michelle seems forced, as though it were part of some larger bargain. Before *A Promised Land* and Michelle's equally florid *Becoming,* the Michelle one met through the media seemed something of a scold and an intimidator, the one who brought the "rage" to the table. "She's a little meaner than I am," Obama joked in a 2007 breakout article in the *New York Times.* "Everyone in the family is afraid of her," brother Craig said in the same article.[419] Observed intimate adviser Valerie Jarrett of their marriage, "There is a subtle element of fear on his part, which is good."[420] Says Michelle of herself in *Becoming,* "When something sets me off, the feeling can be intensely physical, a kind of fireball running up my spine and exploding with such force that I sometimes later don't remember what I said in the moment."[421]

From her days at Princeton forward, Michelle has projected the racial paranoia that many blacks learn as children and never manage to shuck. Although Obama was spared that anxiety, Michelle, like Jackson and Sharpton, was always ready to make her fears seemed justified. Christopher Hitchens sensed Michelle's baleful influence during the 2008 campaign and dared to say so out loud. "All right, then, how is it that the loathsome Wright married him, baptized his children, and received donations from him?" he asked. "Could it possibly have anything, I wonder, to do with Mrs. Obama?"[422] As if to prove Hitchens's point, in *Becoming* Michelle describes Wright as "a sensational preacher with a passion for social justice."[423]

As a candidate Obama worked hard to present himself as an authentic African American, never more painfully so than on one memorable campaign stop in March 2007. Weeks after he declared his candidacy for president, Obama journeyed to Alabama for the annual commemoration of the famed Selma to Montgomery marches of 1965. There he gave a speech, and so did Hillary Clinton. Although Obama's faux black preacher accent was not quite as grating as Hillary's, she didn't claim to be a product of the civil rights movement.

Obama did. As he told the gathered civil rights veterans, the Kennedys launched an airlift in the early 1960s to bring Africans to America to study. "And this young man named Barack Obama," said candidate Obama, "got one of those tickets and came over to this country." Here he met a woman whose distant ancestors owned slaves. "But something stirred across the country because of what happened in Selma, Alabama," said Obama, "because some folks were willing to march across a bridge. And so [my parents] got together, Barack Obama Jr. was born."[424]

Obama either didn't know his history or was confident no one would fact-check him. Obama's mother was already pregnant when Kennedy was elected. At the time of the Selma march, Obama, by any count, was more than three years old. The story he told at Selma was pure hogwash. In *A Promised Land*, he spends several pages on the march. His Selma speech, in fact, provides the essential metaphor for his book. Moses, he told his Selma audience, never got to see "the promised land." That job was left to "the Joshua generation," the American equivalent of which Obama was poised to lead. Regrettably, he fails to address the outrageous mendacity of his Selma speech. Unable or unwilling to tell the truth, he would lead the Joshua generation only to disaster.

Although David Garrow and I view Obama from different political perspectives, we have come to similar conclusions about Obama as man and as president. Writes Garrow: "While he had indeed 'willed himself into being'—as an African American man, as a loving father, and as a successful politician—eight years in the White House had revealed all too clearly that it is easy to forget who you once were if you have never really known who you are."

Obama's failure to know who he really is has had tragic consequences, particularly for black America. In January 2009, the month Obama was inaugurated, 79 percent of whites and 64 percent of blacks held a favorable view of race relations in America.[425] The numbers never got better. By January 2016, when Donald Trump was still a blip on the horizon, 61 percent of blacks were telling Pew that race relations were "generally bad." Only 28 percent of whites and 51 percent of blacks thought Obama had "made progress on race relations." After eight years of a black president and a black attorney general, after eight years of ever more aggressive affirmative action programs, after eight years of widespread inclusiveness and diversity training, only 19 percent of Americans of all races thought race relations were improving.[426]

If We Are Honest
with Ourselves

Late in 2016, the eighth year of the Obama presidency, NFL quarterback Colin Kaepernick took his celebrated knee. Like Obama, the biracial Kaepernick had grown up in a white household, and was, if anything, more confused about his identity than was Obama. Said Kaepernick, forgetting for a minute his twelve-million-dollar salary and his black president, "I am not going to stand up to show pride in a flag for a country that oppresses black people and people of color."

"There are bodies in the street," Kaepernick added, "and people getting paid leave and getting away with murder."[427] There were bodies in the street, but the people who were getting away with murder, for the most part, were the black young men who killed other black young men. Kaepernick's protest gave Obama an excellent opportunity to tell the troubled young athlete what he told the parishioners at the Apostolic Church on Father's Day 2008. *"If we are honest with ourselves,"* said Obama eight years earlier, but honest he never quite managed to be.

In his memoir, Obama does not once use the word "murder" in an American context. Michelle does. In *Becoming*, she laments Chicago's appalling murder rate, adding indignantly, "It goes without saying that nearly all those victims were black."[428] True to form, she makes no mention of who killed them or why. Most of the victims she mentions by name are the ones who were killed by the police or in police custody, including Ferguson's Michael Brown. "All this," she writes, "was evidence of something pernicious and unchanging in America."[429]

Fearing rebuke from more authentic blacks, Michelle included, Obama embraced Sharpton's party line and, as Rudy Giuliani observed, passively encouraged African Americans to direct their rage at law enforcement. With Obama refusing to tell the truth about Trayvon Martin's death, a trio of activists formed Black Lives Matter. With Obama refusing to tell the truth about Michael Brown's death, BLM and its allies intimidated cops into pulling back from active policing. Thugs filled the void, and the murder rate shot up the charts with a bullet. Thanks to the so-called "Ferguson effect," three thousand more people, the majority of them black, were murdered in 2016 than in 2014.

"How many times in the last year has this city lost a child at the hands of another child?" asked Obama at that Chicago church on Father's Day. Well, in 2016, a record 784 people were murdered in Chicago alone, a 57 percent increase over 2015.[430] With Obama out of power, BLM lay low for the next three years, and homicides declined nationwide. But its activists, joined now by Antifa, had mastered the theater of grievance. They exploited the bad optics of chronic felon George Floyd's fentanyl-induced death to radicalize the young and to scare corporate America into further submission.

In his lengthy, feckless tweet following Floyd's death, Obama reminded black Americans that for them, "Being treated differently on account of race is tragically, painfully, maddeningly 'normal.'" Michelle skipped the nuance. "Race and racism is a reality that so many of us grow up learning to just deal with. But if we ever hope to move past it, it can't just be on people of color to deal with it," she tweeted. She then listed, as if martyrs, a string of black people who died resisting arrest all the way back to "Michael," no last name needed.[431]

While America burned, the Obamas found safe harbor in their promised land, Martha's Vineyard. For less fortunate African Americans the cities offered no such sanctuary. Murder in 2020 increased at a shocking 37 percent clip over the year before, the victims and victimizers disproportionately black.[432] Of course, it did not have to be this way. In 2008, America handed Obama an extraordinary opportunity. Had he the courage to repeat his Father's Day address in every relevant venue, he would have forced his followers to understand the source of the pathologies that plagued American cities. Instead, he and Michelle encouraged them to read "race" into every slight, every disparity, every grievance, real or imagined. His cowardice pulled the nation apart and drove the homicide rate upward. Deception was his strategy and division his legacy. Few people will remember TARP or ACA or Dodd-Frank, but no one forgets the murder of a loved one.

Endnotes

1   "Text of Obama's Fatherhood Speech," *Politico*, June 15, 2008, https://www.politico.com/story/2008/06/text-of-obamas-fatherhood-speech-011094.

2   Ibid.

3   Alicia Stanley (Trayvon's stepmom) on Anderson Cooper, June 28 2013, YouTube, https://www.youtube.com/watch?v=4aqS-FfHcy4.

4   Jesse Lee Peterson, *Antidote*: *Healing America from the Poison of Hate, Blame, and Victimhood* (Washington: WND Books, 2015), 38.

5   John Richardson, "Michael Brown Sr. and the Agony of the Black Father in America," *Esquire*, January 5, 2015, https://www.esquire.com/news-politics/interviews/a30808/michael-brown-father-interview-0115/.

6   "Transcript: Barack Obama's Speech on Race," NPR, March 18, 2008, https://www.npr.org/templates/story/story.php?storyId=88478467.

7   Barack Obama, *A Promised Land* (New York: Crown, 2020), Kindle edition, 140–143.

8   Barack Obama, *Dreams from My Father: A Tale of Race and Inheritance* (New York: Three Rivers Press, 1995), 51.

9   Chris Matthews, *Hardball with Chris Matthews*, March 18, 2008, https://www.nbcnews.com/id/wbna23707778.

10   *A Promised Land*, 147.

11   Ibid., 146–147.

12   Ibid.

13   Ibid., 144.

14   Jason Zengerle, "How Barack Obama Sold Out the Kale Crowd," *The New Republic,* April 29, 2014, https://newrepublic.com/article/117504/obama-failed-foodies.

15   *A Promised Land*, 144.

16 "Palin Power: Fresh Face Now More Popular Than Obama, McCain," Rasmussen Reports, September 5, 2008, https://web.archive.org/web/20080906053604/http://www.rasmussenreports.com/public_content/politics/election_20082/2008_presidential_election/palin_power_fresh_face_now_more_popular_than_obama_mccain.

17 *A Promised Land*, 170.

18 Mark Penn, Penn Strategy Memo, March 19, 2007, https://www.scribd.com/doc/4097983/Penn-Strategy-Memo-3-19-07.

19 *A Promised Land*, 169.

20 Jon Swaine, "Who Won the VP Debate: Palin or Joe Biden?" *Telegraph*, October 3, 2008, https://www.telegraph.co.uk/news/newstopics/uselection2008/presidentialdebates/3129259/Who-won-the-VP-debate-Palin-or-Joe-Biden.html.

21 Maeve Reston, "When Romney Trounced Obama," CNN, updated September 26, 2016, https://www.cnn.com/2016/09/25/politics/obama-debate-election-2012/index.html.

22 "Transcript: The Vice-Presidential Debate," *New York Times,* October 2, 2008, https://www.nytimes.com/elections/2008/president/debates/transcripts/vice-presidential-debate.html.

23 *A Promised Land,* 170.

24 Ibid.

25 Ibid., 169.

26 Ibid., 170.

27 Ray LaHood, *Seeking Bipartisanship: My Life in Politics* (Amherst, New York: Cambria Press, 2015), 215.

28 Matt Latimer, "True-Blue Obama," *Politico*, January/February 2016, https://www.politico.com/magazine/story/2016/01/barack-obama-conservative-lament-213491.

29 John Kerry, *Every Day Is Extra* (New York: Simon & Schuster, 2018), Kindle edition, 62.

30 Christopher Andersen, *Barack and Michelle: Portrait of an American Marriage* (New York: HarperCollins eBooks, 2009),144.

31 "A Dubious Compliment," *Time*, January 31, 2007, http://content.time.com/time/specials/packages/article/0,28804,1895156_1894977_1644536,00.html.

32 *A Promised Land,* 51.

33 "Barack Obama's Remarks to the Democratic National Convention," *New York Times,* July 27, 2004, https://www.nytimes.com/2004/07/27/politics/campaign/barack-obamas-remarks-to-the-democratic-national.html.

34 "Chimamanda Ngozi Adichie on Barack Obama's 'A Promised Land,'" *New York Times,* November 12, 2020, https://www.nytimes.com/2020/11/12/books/review/barack-obama-a-promised-land.html.

35 *A Promised Land,* 246.

36 Ibid.

37 Ibid.

38 Ibid., 506.

39 Ibid., 152.

40 Ibid., 153.

41 Ibid.

42 Ibid., 672.

43 Ibid., 194.

44 Ibid., 210.

45 Michael Eric Dyson, "The Ghost of Cornel West," *New Republic,* April 19, 2015, https://newrepublic.com/article/121550/cornel-wests-rise-fall-our-most-exciting-black-scholar-ghost.

46 Vincent Canby, "Film: 'Zelig,' Woody Allen's Story about a 'Chameleon Man,'" *New York Times,* July 16, 1983, https://www.nytimes.com/1983/07/15/movies/film-zelig-woody-allen-s-story-about-a-chameleon-man-034845.html.

47 David Garrow, *Rising Star: The Making of Barack Obama* (New York, William Morrow, 2017), Kindle edition, location 3663.

48 Penn Strategy Memo.

49 Berg v. Obama, FindLaw, https://caselaw.findlaw.com/us-3rd-circuit/1498770.html.

50 Philip Berg, *ObamaScare* (Berwick, PA: Shecktor Enterprises, 2015), Kindle edition, 94.

51 Ibid., 116.

52 Ibid., 149.

53 *A Promised Land,* 195.

54 Stephen Glass, "Spring Breakdown," *New Republic,* March 31, 1997, http://wp.lps.org/akabour/files/2013/12/Spring-Breakdown-Stephen-Glass.pdf.

55 "Donald Trump Remarks," C-SPAN, February 10, 2011, https://www.c-span.org/video/?297952-12/donald-trump-remarks.

56 Ibid.

57 *A Promised Land,* 672.

58 Ibid., 301.

59 Ibid.

60 Ibid., 411.

61 *Rising Star,* 2369–2375.

62   *A Promised Land*, 275.

63   David Remnick, *The Bridge: The Life and Rise of Barack Obama* (New York: Vintage Books, 2010), Kindle edition, 235–239.

64   Ibid., 56.

65   *A Promised Land*, 674.

66   John McKnight, "My Student Barack Obama," *Inclusion*, January 12, 2020, https://inclusion.com/2020/john-mcknight-my-student-barack-obama/.

67   *Dreams*, 149.

68   *The Bridge*, 187.

69   Vernon Jarrett, "Will Arabs Back Ties to Blacks with Cash?" *St. Petersburg Independent*, November 6, 1979, 19-a, https://news.google.com/newspapers?nid=950&dat=19791106&id=RcFaAAAAIBAJ&sjid=GFkDAAAAIBAJ&pg=6597,1456637&hl=en.

70   *A Promised Land*, 672.

71   *Barack and Michelle*, 176.

72   Liza Mundy, *Michelle: A Biography* (New York: Simon & Schuster, 2008), 64.

73   Michelle Obama, *Becoming* (New York: Crown, 2018), Kindle edition, 62.

74   Ibid., 67.

75   Ibid., 78.

76   Christopher Hitchens, "Are We Getting Two for One?" *Slate*, May 5, 2008, https://slate.com/news-and-politics/2008/05/is-michelle-obama-responsible-for-the-jeremiah-wright-fiasco.html.

77   Michelle LaVaughn Robinson, "Princeton-Educated Blacks and the Black Community," Princeton University, 1985, https://www.politico.com/pdf/080222_MOPrincetonThesis_1-251.pdf.

78   *Becoming*, 74.

79   Ibid., 91.

80   *A Promised Land*, 18.

81   Shelby Steele, *A Bound Man: Why We Are Excited About Obama and Why He Can't Win* (New York: Free Press, 2007), 14.

82   *A Promised Land*, 19.

83   *Rising Star*, 8419–8459.

84   *A Promised Land*, 274.

85   Jan Ransom, "Trump Will Not Apologize for Calling for Death Penalty Over Central Park Five," *New York Times*, June 18, 2019, https://www.nytimes.com/2019/06/18/nyregion/central-park-five-trump.html.

86   David Pitt, "Joggers Attackers Terrorized at Least 9 in 2 Hours," *New York Times*, April 22, 1989, https://www.nytimes.com/1989/04/22/nyregion/jogger-s-attackers-terrorized-at-least-9-in-2-hours.html.

87 Lisa W. Foderaro, "Angered by Attack, Trump Urges Return of the Death Penalty," *New York Times,* May 1, 1989, https://www.nytimes.com/1989/05/01/nyregion/angered-by-attack-trump-urges-return-of-the-death-penalty.html.

88 Joel Pollak, "Exclusive—Obama's Literary Agent in 1991 Booklet: 'Born in Kenya and Raised in Indonesia and Hawaii,'" Breitbart, May 17, 2012, https://www.breitbart.com/politics/2012/05/17/The-Vetting-Barack-Obama-Literary-Agent-1991-Born-in-Kenya-Raised-Indonesia-Hawaii/.

89 *A Promised Land,* 675.

90 Ibid., 674.

91 Penn Strategy Memo.

92 Ibid.

93 *Dreams,* 7.

94 "Complete Text of the President's Speech to School Children," September 8, 2009, Fox19 Now, https://www.fox19.com/story/11088721/complete-text-of-the-presidents-speech-to-school-children/.

95 Lewis Carroll, *Alice in Wonderland,* Open Books, 125, http://www.open-bks.com/alice-125-126.html.

96 "Barack Obama's Remarks to the Democratic National Convention," July 27, 2004.

97 "Malik Obama Interviewed by Director Joel Gilbert," YouTube, April 22, 2015, https://www.youtube.com/watch?v=eRKVunuTGDQ&feature=youtu.be.

98 *Dreams,* 234.

99 *A Promised Land,* 132.

100 "Malik Obama Interviewed by Director Joel Gilbert."

101 *The Bridge,* 360.

102 Rebecca Mead, "Obama, Poet," *New Yorker,* June 25, 2007, https://www.newyorker.com/magazine/2007/07/02/obama-poet.

103 *Rising Star,* 2936–2939.

104 Cliff Kincaid, Accuracy in Media, March 23, 2019.

105 *A Promised Land,* 125.

106 Annie Karni and Glenn Thrush, "Bill Clinton Seeks Redemption in South Carolina," *Politico,* February 26, 2016, https://www.politico.com/story/2016/02/bill-clinton-south-carolina-redemption-219811.

107 Penn Strategy Memo.

108 *A Promised Land,* 113.

109 *Rising Star,* 1076–1078

110 Ibid., 1221–1222.

111 Janny Scott, *A Singular Woman: The Untold Story of Barack Obama's Mother* (New York: Riverhead Books, 2011), 84.

112 David Maraniss, *Barack Obama: The Story* (New York: Simon & Schuster, 2012), Kindle edition, 175.

113 Chimamanda Ngozi Adichie, "Chimamanda Ngozi Adichie on Barack Obama's 'A Promised Land,'" *New York Times*, November 12, 2020, https://www.nytimes.com/2020/11/12/books/review/barack-obama-a-promised-land.html.

114 Carlos Lozada, "The Examined Life of Barack Obama," *Washington Post*, November 17, 2020, https://www.washingtonpost.com/outlook/2020/11/17/obama-promised-land-memoir-autobiography/?arc404=true.

115 Jennifer Szalai, "In 'A Promised Land,' Barack Obama Thinks—and Thinks Some More—Over His First Term," *New York Times*, November 15, 2020, https://www.nytimes.com/2020/11/15/books/review-barack-obama-promised-land-memoir.html.

116 Ibid., 703.

117 *A Promised Land*, 674.

118 Ibid., 132.

119 Ibid., 57.

120 *Rising Star*, 23069–23070.

121 "Transcript: Obama and Clinton Debate," ABC News, April 16, 2008, https://abcnews.go.com/Politics/DemocraticDebate/story?id=4670271&page=1.

122 *Rising Star*, 11190 and following.

123 *The Bridge*, 253.

124 David Garrow, "Obama's Airbrushed Dreams," *The Critic*, March 2020, https://thecritic.co.uk/issues/march-2020/obamas-airbrushed-dreams/.

125 *Barack and Michelle*, 135.

126 Jack Cashill, *Deconstructing Obama: The Life, Loves and Letters of America's First Postmodern President* (New York: Simon & Schuster, 2011), 105–106.

127 *Rising Star*, 11976.

128 *Dreams*, 139.

129 *A Promised Land*, 118.

130 Valerie Strauss and Bill Turque, "Fate of D.C. Voucher Program Darkens," *Washington Post*, June 9, 2008, https://www.washingtonpost.com/wp-dyn/content/article/2008/06/08/AR2008060802041.html?hpid=topnews.

131 *A Promised Land*, 265.

132 Roland S. Martin, "Commentary: Obama, Dems Wrong to Kill School Vouchers," CNN Politics, March 11, 2009, https://www.cnn.com/2009/POLITICS/03/11/martin.vouchers/index.html.

133 Lindsey Burke, "Obama's Budget Ends Funding for D.C. Opportunity Scholarship Program," *Daily Signal*, February 13, 2012, https://www.

dailysignal.com/2012/02/13/presidents-budget-eliminates-funding-for-d-c-opportunity-scholarship-program/.

134 *A Promised Land*, 672.

135 "Obama's Budget Ends Funding for D.C. Opportunity Scholarship Program," *Daily Signal*.

136 *Dreams*, 49.

137 *Rising Star*, 11772–11777.

138 Ibid, 11799.

139 "Obama Rally in Richmond, Virginia," October 22, 2008, https://www.c-span.org/video/?281938-1/obama-rally-richmond-virginia.

140 Jonathan Raban, "All the Presidents' Literature," *Wall Street Journal*, January 10, 2009, https://www.wsj.com/articles/SB123154076720569453.

141 *Rising Star*, 10959.

142 Ibid., 9785–9860.

143 Barack Obama, "Breaking the War Mentality," *Sundial*, March 1983, http://www.columbia.edu/cu/computinghistory/obama-sundial.pdf.

144 *Barack and Michelle*, 134.

145 *Rising Star*, 10966–10967.

146 *Barack Obama: The Story*, 566.

147 Ibid.

148 Jack Cashill, "Obama's Apocryphal Kenya Trip," *American Thinker*, January 14, 2014, http://66.226.135.81/intellect_fraud/obamas_apocryphal_kenya.htm.

149 Rashid Khalidi, *Resurrecting Empire: Western Footprints and America's Perilous Path in the Middle East* (Boston: Beacon Press, 2005), 212.

150 Viveca Novak, "Bum Rap for Rahm," FactCheck.org, January 13, 2011, https://www.factcheck.org/2011/01/bum-rap-for-rahm/.

151 Jennifer Szalai, *New York Times*.

152 *A Promised Land*, 177.

153 "Barack Obama's Speech at Nasdaq," *New York Times*, September 17, 2007, https://www.nytimes.com/2007/09/17/us/politics/16text-obama.html.

154 Paul Sperry, *The Great American Bank Robbery* (Google Books, 2011), 38.

155 John McKnight, "Two Kinds of Community Organizing," Abundant Community, July 7, 2010, https://www.abundantcommunity.com/two-kinds-of-community-organizing-2/.

156 "Interview, Gerald Kellamn," *Frontline*, PBS, October 14, 2008, https://www.pbs.org/wgbh/pages/frontline/choice2008/interviews/kellman.html.

157 Serge Kovaleski, "Obama's Organizing Years, Guiding Others and Finding Himself," *New York Times*, July 7, 2008, https://www.nytimes.com/2008/07/07/us/politics/07community.html.

158 Barack Obama, "Why Organize?" *After Alinsky: Community Organizing in Illinois*, 1990, *http://garifunacoalition.org/yahoo_site_admin/assets/docs/WhyOrganize-BarackObama.143111756.pdf*.

159 *A Promised Land*, 195.

160 Leslie Wayne, "Fading Red Line; A Special Report; New Hope in Inner Cities: Banks Offering Mortgages," *New York Times*, March 14, 1992, https://www.nytimes.com/1992/03/14/business/fading-red-line-special-report-new-hope-inner-cities-banks-offering-mortgages.html.

161 Ibid.

162 Stephanie Strom, "On Obama, Acorn, and Voter Registration," *New York Times*, October 10, 2008, https://www.nytimes.com/2008/10/11/us/politics/11acorn.html?_r=0.

163 "Palin Criticizes Obama over ACORN, View of America," KFDA 10, October 16, 2008, https://www.newschannel10.com/story/9191241/palin-criticizes-obama-over-acorn-view-of-america/.

164 *A Promised Land*, 195.

165 "Children Suffer as Single-Parenting Rates Soar in Chicago and Across the U.S.," Smart Library on Urban Poverty, https://www.coursehero.com/file/p5lt42n/because-black-children-are-far-more-likely-to-live-in-single-parent-families/.

166 Thomas Sowell, *The Housing Boom and Bust* (New York: Basic Books, 2009), 97–99.

167 "Analysis of FHA Single-Family Default and Loss Rates," *HUD User Publications*, March 2004.

168 Selma S. Buycks-Roberson et al. v. Citibank Federal Savings Bank, Settlement Agreement, January 9, 1998, https://www.clearinghouse.net/chDocs/public/FH-IL-0011-0008.pdf.

169 Wade Rathke, "Different Days on Park Avenue with Citibank," *Chief Organizer Blog*, April 1, 2004, https://chieforganizer.org/2004/04/01/different-days-on-park-avenue-with-citibank/.

170 Ibid.

171 Janet Hook and Dan Morain, "Democrats Are Darlings of Wall St.," *Los Angeles Times*, March 21, 2008, https://www.latimes.com/archives/la-xpm-2008-mar-21-na-wallstdems21-story.html.

172 "First Union Capital Markets Corp., Bear, Stearns & Co. Price Securities Offering Backed by Affordable Mortgages," press release, October 20, 1997.

173 Michael Lewis, "A Wall Street Trader Draws Some Subprime Lessons," Bloomberg News, September 5, 2007.

174 "Full Text of President Clinton's Speech," *CBS News*, August 14, 2000, https://www.cbsnews.com/news/full-text-of-president-clintons-speech/.

175 "HUD Announces New Regulations to Provide $2.4 Trillion in Mortgages for Affordable Housing for 28.1 Million Families," HUD news press release, October 31, 2000.

176 Wayne Barrett, "Andrew Cuomo and Fannie and Freddie: How the Youngest Housing and Urban Development Secretary in History Gave Birth to the Mortgage Crisis," *Village Voice*, August 5, 2008.

177 Thomas Sowell, *The Housing Boom and Bust* (New York: Basic Books, 209), 41–42.

178 "Full Transcript: The Vice-Presidential Debate," *New York Times*, May 23, 2012, https://www.nytimes.com/2012/10/11/us/politics/full-transcript-of-the-vice-presidential-debate.html.

179 *A Promised Land*, 38.

180 *Becoming*, 150.

181 Ibid., 158.

182 *Barack and Michelle*, 292.

183 *A Promised Land*, 273.

184 *The Housing Boom and Bust*, 53.

185 Ibid., 50–51.

186 "Barney Frank in 2005: What Housing Bubble?" YouTube.com, June 27, 2005, https://www.youtube.com/watch?feature=endscreen&NR=1&v=iW5qKYfqALE.

187 *A Promised Land*, 188.

188 Ibid., 174.

189 *The Great American Bank Robbery*, 61–62.

190 Adam Michelson, *The Foreclosure of America: The Inside Story of the Rise and Fall of Countrywide Home Loans, the Mortgage Crisis, and the Default of the American Dream* (New York: Berkley Books, 2009), 270–72.

191 Michael Lewis, "The Man Who Crashed the World," *Vanity Fair*, June 10, 2009, https://www.vanityfair.com/news/2009/06/the-man-who-crashed-the-world.

192 "Transcript: Barack Obama's Acceptance Speech," NPR, August 28, 2008, https://www.npr.org/templates/story/story.php?storyId=94087570.

193 Blake Hounshell, "Palin 'Disappointed' by AIG Bailout," *Foreign Policy*, September 17, 2008, https://foreignpolicy.com/2008/09/17/palin-disappointed-by-aig-bailout/.

194 *A Promised Land*, 193.

195 Ibid., 291.

196 Ibid., 304.

197 Dan Eggen, "Obama Campaign Attracts Wall Street Money, Despite Tensions," *Washington Post,* July 22, 2011, https://www.washingtonpost.com/politics/obama-campaign-attracts-wall-street-money-despite-tensions/2011/07/22/gIQApIugTI_story.html.

198 *A Promised Land,* 260.

199 Ibid., 261.

200 David Schulman, *Sons of Wichita: How the Koch Brothers Became America's Most Forceful and Private Dynasty* (New York: Grand Central Publishing, 2014), 272–274.

201 *A Promised Land,* 257.

202 Ibid., 258.

203 "Transcript from *Meet the Press,*" *Politico,* December 7, 2008, https://www.politico.com/story/2008/12/transcript-from-meet-the-press-016278.

204 "Full Text of Obama's Speech to Congress and the Nation," *Los Angeles Times,* February 24, 2009, https://latimesblogs.latimes.com/washington/2009/02/obama-text-spee.html.

205 "Obama's Economic Speech," FactCheck.org, December 8, 2009, https://www.factcheck.org/2009/12/obamas-economic-speech/.

206 Peter Baker, "Education of a President," *New York Times,* October 12, 2010, https://www.nytimes.com/2010/10/17/magazine/17obama-t.html?_r=4&ref=magazine&pagewanted=all%22&.

207 "Transcript from *Meet the Press,*" *Politico,* December 7, 2008, https://www.politico.com/story/2008/12/transcript-from-meet-the-press-016278.

208 "100 Stimulus Projects: A Second Opinion," Sen. Tom Coburn, June 2009, https://coburn.library.okstate.edu/pdf/100_stimulus_projects_a_second_opinion.pdf.

209 *A Promised Land,* 265.

210 "Transcript and Audio: First Obama-Romney Debate," NPR, October 3, 2012, https://www.npr.org/2012/10/03/162258551/transcript-first-obama-romney-presidential-debate.

211 *Tavis Smiley,* PBS, April 20, 2009.

212 Christopher Dodd, "Mortgage Market Turmoil: Causes and Consequences," opening statement before US Senate Committee on Banking, Housing, and Urban Affairs, March 22, 2007.

213 *A Promised Land,* 556.

214 Glenn Thrush, "Trump Vows to Dismantle Dodd-Frank 'Disaster,'" *New York Times,* January 30, 2017, https://www.nytimes.com/2017/01/30/us/politics/trump-dodd-frank-regulations.html.

215 Jesse Solomon, "Bloomberg Slams Dodd-Frank, Obamacare," CNN Business, November 10, 2014, https://money.cnn.com/2014/11/10/investing/bloomber g-financial-regulation-obamacare/index.html.

216 J. D. Harrison, "Dodd-Frank's Regulatory Nightmare in One Rather Mesmerizing Illustration," US Chamber of Commerce, May 9, 2016, https://www.uschamber.com/series/above-the-fold/dodd-frank-s-regulatory-nightmar e-one-rather-mesmerizing-illustration.

217 Maggie Haberman and Nicholas Fandos, "Trump and Pence Push the Chamber of Commerce on Democratic Endorsements," *New York Times*, September 18, 2020, https://www.nytimes.com/2020/09/18/us/elections/trum p-and-pence-push-the-chamber-of-commerce-on-democratic-endorsements. html.

218 Hans Spakovsky and Alden Abbot, "A Win for Separation of Powers? Court Rules Against Consumer Financial Protection Bureau," Heritage Foundation, November 4, 2016, https://www.heritage.org/economic-and-property-rights/ commentary/win-separation-powers-court-rules-against-consumer.

219 *A Promised Land*, 556.

220 AnnaMaria Andriotis and Rachel Louise Ensign, "U.S. Government Uses Race Test for $80 Million in Payments," *Wall Street Journal,* October 29, 2015, https://www.wsj.com/articles/u-s-uses-race-test-to-decide-who-to-pay-in-ally-auto-loan-pact-1446111002?mod=grfx.

221 *A Promised Land,* 554.

222 Ibid., 68.

223 Ibid., 129.

224 Michael Kelly, "Ted Kennedy on the Rocks," *Esquire*, February 1, 1990, https://www.gq.com/story/kennedy-ted-senator-profile.

225 "Michelle Obama Says 'Access Hollywood' Tape Prompted Her to Condemn Trump's Comments," *PBS Newshour,* November 16, 2018, https://www.pbs. org/newshour/politics/michelle-obama-says-access-hollywood-tape-prompted-her-to-condemn-trumps-comments.

226 *Becoming*, 407.

227 *A Promised Land*, 50.

228 Ben Wallace-Wells, "Obama's Narrator," *New York Times*, April 1, 2007, https://www.nytimes.com/2007/04/01/magazine/01axelrod.t.html.

229 Michael Martinez and Rick Pearson, "Court Sets Release of Ryan's Divorce File," *Chicago Tribune*, June 18, 2004, https://www.chicagotribune.com/ chi-0406180364jun18-story.html.

230 *Becoming*, 213.

231 Tara Reade, "A Girl Walks into the Senate," *The Union*, April 17, 2019, https://www.theunion.com/opinion/columns/alexandra-tara-reade-a-girl-walks-into-the-senate/.

232 "The Tara Reade Interview: Accusing Joe Biden of Sexual Assault," *60 Minutes Australia*, October 4, 2020, https://www.youtube.com/watch?v=OOti0PJl J7A&fbclid=IwAR1XoTwo5Gi2FgSIvFBLE84H9hdqDVez9_wTXbf39Ry9o JCu_X8ak6I1iy0.

233 *A Promised Land,* 259.

234 "No Means No," YouTube, March 16, 2017, https://www.youtube.com/watch?v=vwam-tgdwas.

235 *A Promised Land,* 163.

236 Garrow, *Rising Star,* (paperback edition, 2019), 113.

237 Email from David Garrow, January 17, 2020.

238 Jennifer Schuessler, "His Martin Luther King Biography Was a Classic. His Latest King Piece Is Causing a Furor," *New York Times*, June 4, 2019, https://www.nytimes.com/2019/06/04/arts/king-fbi-tapes-david-garrow.html.

239 *A Promised Land,* 132.

240 *Dreams,* 115.

241 *Rising Star,* 23740–23744.

242 Ibid., 23318.

243 Ibid., 23542–23545.

244 *A Promised Land,* 589.

245 Ben Ashford, "EXCLUSIVE: Baggies of Crystal Meth, Empty Corona Bottles and Soiled Bedding: These Are the Sordid Images of the Raucous Hotel Party That Sent Florida Dem Andrew Gillum to Rehab and Left Male Escort Hospitalized," *Daily Mail*, March 20, 2020, https://www.dailymail.co.uk/news/article-8134995/Inside-hotel-room-married-Florida-Dem-Andrew-Gillum-overdosed-male-escort.html.

246 Sofia Petkar, "College Sweetheart: Who Is Andrew Gillum's Wife R. Jai Gillum?" *The Sun*, September 15, 2020, https://www.the-sun.com/news/1472510/andrew-gillum-wife-r-jai-bisexual-democrat/.

247 Benoit Denizet-Lewis, "Double Lives on the Down Low," *New York Times Magazine*, August 3, 2003, https://www.nytimes.com/2003/08/03/magazine/double-lives-on-the-down-low.html.

248 *A Promised Land,* 610.

249 Ibid., 132.

250 "Larry Sinclair Press Conference Exposing Barack Obama," YouTube, May 17, 2012, https://www.youtube.com/watch?v=3QK0eGp3N6A.

251 "Saddleback Civil Forum on the Presidency," August 16, 2008, http://www. thirty-thousand.org/pages/Saddleback_16AUG2008.htm.

252 Sarah Posner, "Rick Warren Proposition 8 Endorsement Further Explodes the 'New Evangelical' Myth," *The American Prospect,* October 24, 2008, https://prospect.org/article/rick-warren-proposition-8-endorsement-explodes-new-evangelical-myth./.

253 Chris Cillizza and Sean Sullivan, "How Proposition 8 Passed in California— and Why It Wouldn't Today," *Washington Post,* March 26, 2013, https://www. washingtonpost.com/news/the-fix/wp/2013/03/26/how-proposition-8-passed-in-california-and-why-it-wouldnt-today/.

254 Bil Browning, "Today Is *the Day* but I'm Angry Instead," *The Bilerico Project,* November 5, 2008, http://bilerico.lgbtqnation.com/2008/11/today_is_the_day_but_im_angry_instead.php.

255 Joe Sudbay, "Transcript of Q and A with the President about DADT and Same-Sex Marriage," *Americablog,* March 27, 2010, https://gay.americablog. com/2010/10/transcript-of-q-and-a-with-the-president-about-dadt-and-same-sex-marriage.html.

256 Audrey Bilger, "Obama Evolves!" *Ms.,* May 9, 2012, https://msmagazine. com/2012/05/09/obama-evolves/.

257 *Rising Star,* 12299–12300.

258 "Transcript of Q and A with the President about DADT and Same-Sex Marriage."

259 *A Promised Land,* 404.

260 "Transcript of Second McCain, Obama Debate," CNN Politics, October 7, 2008, https://www.cnn.com/2008/POLITICS/10/07/presidential.debate. transcript/.

261 D'Angelo Gore, "Obama's Untrue Anecdote," FactCheck.org, July 14, 2011, https://www.factcheck.org/2011/07/obamas-untrue-anecdote/.

262 *A Promised Land,* 87.

263 Ibid., 411.

264 "Obama's Speech on Health Care Reform," *New York Times,* June 15, 2009, https://www.nytimes.com/2009/06/15/health/policy/15obama.text. html?pagewanted=3&_r=0.

265 Patrick Howley, "Obamacare Architect: Lack of Transparency Was Key Because 'Stupidity of the American Voter' Would Have Killed Obamacare," *Daily Caller,* November 9, 2014, https://theridgewoodblog.net/nj/stupidity-of-voter/.

266 *A Promised Land,* 424.

267 Tabitha Hale, "Stupak: HHS Mandate Violates My Obamacare Compromise," Breitbart, September 4, 2012, https://www.breitbart.com/politics/2012/09/04/Stupak-President-Played-Me-with-Obamacare-Deal/.

268 "Induced Abortion in the United States," Guttmacher Institute, https://www.guttmacher.org/fact-sheet/induced-abortion-united-states.

269 *A Promised Land*, 426.

270 "Alice Palmer," Discover the Networks, https://www.discoverthenetworks.org/individuals/alice-palmer/.

271 *A Promised Land*, 28.

272 Ibid., 29.

273 Ibid.

274 *Rising Star*, 12278–12309.

275 "Barack Obama 2020 60 Minutes Interview Transcript," Rev, November 15, 2020, https://www.rev.com/blog/transcripts/barack-obama-2020-60-minutes-interview-transcript.

276 "Interview with Sarah Palin by Sean Hannity on Fox News' 'Hannity & Colmes,'" The American Presidency Project, October 8, 2008, https://www.presidency.ucsb.edu/documents/interview-with-sarah-palin-sean-hannity-fox-news-hannity-colmes.

277 *A Promised Land,* 195.

278 Ibid., 359.

279 Mark Christian, *The Apostate*, yet to be published.

280 *A Promised Land*, 361.

281 Ibid., 360.

282 Ibid., 588.

283 Ibid., 344

284 Ibid.

285 Ibid., 47.

286 "Fact Check: Did Obama Say the Iraq Troop 'Surge' Would Not Work?" *Political Ticker,* September 26, 2008, https://politicalticker.blogs.cnn.com/2008/09/26/fact-check-did-obama-say-the-iraq-troop-surge-could-not-work/.

287 "Five Days of the Obama ACORN Connection," press releases from McCain-Palin 2008, October 20, 2008, http://p2008.org/mccain/mccain102008pr.html.

288 James O'Keefe, *Breakthrough: Our Guerilla War to Expose Fraud and Save Democracy* (New York: Threshold Editions, 2013), 73.

289 *A Promised Land*, 405.

290 Ibid., 405.

291 Ibid., 406.

292 "Inappropriate Criteria Were Used to Identify Tax-Exempt Applications for Review," Treasury Inspector General, May 14, 2013, https://www.treasury.gov/tigta/auditreports/2013reports/201310053fr.pdf.

293 "Testimony of Catherine Engelbrecht, House Committee on Oversight & Government Reform," February 6, 2014, https://republicans-oversight.house.gov/wp-content/uploads/2014/02/Engelbrecht.pdf.

294 Kerry Picket, "AUDIO: Origin of Rep. Carson's Racism Accusation toward Health Care Protesters," *Washington Times*, April 6, 2010, https://www.washingtontimes.com/blog/watercooler/2010/apr/6/audio-rep-carson-first-peddles-out-racism-story-re/.

295 "Video Proof: The NAACP Rewards Racism," Breitbart, July 19, 2010, https://www.breitbart.com/politics/2010/07/19/video-proof-the-naacp-awards-racism-2010/.

296 Sharon LaFraniere, "U.S. Opens Spigot After Farmers Claim Discrimination," *New York Times*, April 26, 2013, https://www.nytimes.com/2013/04/26/us/farm-loan-bias-claims-often-unsupported-cost-us-millions.html.

297 "Megyn Kelly Interviews Renowned Civil Rights Attorney Bartle Bull," Fox News, July 2, 2010, https://www.youtube.com/watch?v=Vn6h-xeXwcM.

298 J. Christian Adams, "Inside the Black Panther Case," *Washington Times*, June 25, 2010, https://www.washingtontimes.com/news/2010/jun/25/inside-the-black-panther-case-anger-ignorance-and-/.

299 Megyn Kelly interview.

300 Chris Matthews, "And That's the Way It Was," *New York Times*, June 6, 2012, https://www.nytimes.com/2012/07/08/books/review/cronkite-a-biography-by-douglas-brinkley.html.

301 Jessica Chasmar, "Katie Couric Slammed After Saying Members of Trump 'Cult' Need to Be 'Deprogrammed,'" January 19, 2021, https://www.washingtontimes.com/news/2021/jan/19/katie-couric-slammed-after-saying-members-of-trump/.

302 Ibid.

303 *A Promised Land, 242.*

304 Ibid., 407.

305 Ibid., 674.

306 Ibid., 633.

307 Ibid., 276.

308 Ibid., 585.

309 Ibid., 586.

310 Ibid., 666.

311 Ibid., 668.

312 "Remarks by the President in Address to the Nation on Libya," White House, March 28, 2011, https://obamawhitehouse.archives.gov/the-press-office/2011/03/28/remarks-president-address-nation-libya.

313 Alan J. Kuperman, "False Pretense for War in Libya?" *Boston Globe*, April 14, 2011, http://archive.boston.com/bostonglobe/editorial_opinion/oped/articles/2011/04/14/false_pretense_for_war_in_libya/.

314 *A Promised Land*, 256.

315 Ibid., 218.

316 Ibid., 634.

317 Ibid., 341.

318 Ibid., 668.

319 Joe Lieberman, "The Absence of U.S. Leadership Makes the World More Dangerous Than Ever," *Washington Post,* February 24, 2016, https://www.washingtonpost.com/opinions/the-absence-of-us-leadership-makes-the-world-more-dangerous-than-ever/2016/02/24/65e586a8-d8ac-11e5-925f-1d10062cc82d_story.html.

320 *A Promised Land*, 191.

321 Dov Lipman, "Obama's Revisionist 'Promised Land,'" *Jewish Press*, November 27, 2020, https://www.jewishpress.com/indepth/opinions/obamas-revisionist-promised-land/2020/11/27/.

322 Sean Durns, "A Promised Land: Obama's Memoirs Malign Israel," CAMERA, December 15, 2020, https://www.camera.org/article/obamas-memoirs-malign-israel/.

323 Gil Troy, "President-Elect Joe Biden and His New Team Should Correct Obama's Mistakes, Not Repeat Them," *Jerusalem Post*, December 1, 2020, https://www.jpost.com/opinion/obamas-memoir-the-anatomy-of-iran-appeasers-and-bash-israel-firsters-650849.

324 *Rising Star*, 18317.

325 *A Promised Land,* 629.

326 Ibid., 628.

327 Ibid., 8.

328 Ibid., 626.

329 "Obama's Revisionist 'Promised Land,'" *Jewish Press*.

330 *A Promised Land*, 632–634.

331 Ibid., 636.

332 "Obama's Revisionist 'Promised Land,'" *Jewish Press*.

333 *A Promised Land*, 591.

334 Nick Miroff, "'Kids in Cages': It's True That Obama Built the Cages at the Border. But Trump's 'Zero Tolerance' Immigration Policy Had No Precedent," *Washington Post,* October 23, 2020, https://www.washingtonpost.com/immigration/kids-in-cages-debate-trump-obama/2020/10/23/8ff96f3c-1532-11eb-82af-864652063d61_story.html.

335 *A Promised Land,* 616.

336 Ashley Southall, "Obama Vows to Push Immigration Changes," *New York Times,* October 25, 2010, https://thecaucus.blogs.nytimes.com/2010/10/25/in-appeal-to-hispanics-obama-promises-to-push-immigration-reform/.

337 Ibid., 590.

338 Ibid., 603.

339 "Remarks by the President at Univision Town Hall," Obama White House Archives, March 28, 2011, https://obamawhitehouse.archives.gov/the-press-office/2011/03/28/remarks-president-univision-town-hall.

340 "Remarks by the President on Immigration," White House, June 15, 2012, https://obamawhitehouse.archives.gov/the-press-office/2012/06/15/remarks-president-immigration.

341 Dan Hammes, "Geez, he really did stop the oceans," *The Livingston Enterprise,* September 4, 2019, https://www.livingstonenterprise.com/content/geez-he-really-did-stop-oceans.

342 "Barack Obama's Remarks in St. Paul," *New York Times,* June 3, 2008, https://www.nytimes.com/2008/06/03/us/politics/03text-obama.html.

343 *A Promised Land,* 488.

344 Ibid.

345 Ibid., 348.

346 Ellen Goodman, "No Change in Political Climate," *Boston Globe,* February 8, 2017, http://archive.boston.com/news/globe/editorial_opinion/oped/articles/2007/02/09/no_change_in_political_climate/.

347 Iselin Medhaug et al., "Reconciling Controversies about the 'Global Warming Hiatus,'" *Nature,* May 4, 2017, https://www.nature.com/articles/nature22315.

348 Peter Baker and Jeff Zeleny, "For Obama, an Unsuccessful Campaign," *New York Times,* October 2, 2009, https://www.nytimes.com/2009/10/03/sports/03obama.html.

349 *A Promised Land,* 510.

350 Ibid., 504.

351 Tim Grieve and Louise Roug, "Climategate Distracts at Copenhagen," *Politico,* December 9, 2009, https://www.politico.com/story/2009/12/climategate-distracts-at-copenhagen-030406.

352 Ibid.

353 *A Promised Land*, 590.

354 "Obama: My Plan Makes Electricity Rates Skyrocket," YouTube, March 18, 2009, https://www.youtube.com/watch?v=HlTxGHn4sH4.

355 Katelyn Sabochik, "We've Got to Go Back to Making Things," White House, May 26, 2010, https://obamawhitehouse.archives.gov/blog/2010/05/26/we-ve-got-go-back-making-things.

356 *A Promised Land*, 493.

357 Fred Barbash and Harry Siegel, "Van Jones Resigns amid Controversy," *Politico*, September 6, 2009, https://www.politico.com/story/2009/09/van-jones-resigns-amid-controversy-026797.

358 "Full 2012 Town Hall Presidential Debate," YouTube, October 17, 2012, https://www.youtube.com/watch?v=Mc0P5sZzlo0.

359 *A Promised Land*, 684.

360 Ibid.

361 Letter to Loretta J. Fuddy from Judith L. Corley on behalf of President Obama, Obama White House Archives, April 22, 2011, https://obamawhitehouse. archives.gov/sites/default/files/rss_viewer/birth-certificate-correspondence.pdf.

362 "Remarks by the President," White House, April 27, 2011, https://obamawhite-house.archives.gov/the-press-office/2011/04/27/remarks-president.

363 *A Promised Land*, 685.

364 Kia Makarechi, "The Time Obama Edited a White House Correspondents' Dinner Joke," *Vanity F air*, April 22, 2015, https://www.vanityfair.com/news/2015/04/obama-bin-laden-joke-edit-whcd.

365 *A Promised Land*, 692.

366 Kori Schulman, "'The President's Speech' at the White House Correspondents' Dinner," May 1, 2011, https://obamawhitehouse.archives.gov/blog/2011/05/01/president-s-speech-white-house-correspondents-dinner.

367 *A Promised Land*, 692.

368 Leon Panetta, *Worthy Fights: A Memoir of Leadership in War and Peace* (New York: Penguin, 2014), 320.

369 Roxanne Roberts, *Washington Post*, "I Sat Next to Donald Trump at the Infamous 2011 White House Correspondents' Dinner," April 28, 2016, https://www.washingtonpost.com/lifestyle/style/i-sat-next-to-donald-trump-at-the-infamous-2011-white-house-correspondents-dinner/2016/04/27/5cf46b74-0bea-11e6-8ab8-9ad050f76d7d_story.html.

370 *A Promised Land*, 692.

371 Ibid., 695.

372 "Press Briefing by Press Secretary Jay Carney and Assistant to the President for Homeland Security and Counterterrorism John Brennan," May 2, 2011, White

House, https://obamawhitehouse.archives.gov/the-press-office/2011/05/02/press-briefing-press-secretary-jay-carney-and-assistant-president-homela.

373 *Worthy Fights*, 326.

374 Sharyl Attkisson, "Obama on 'Gunwalking': Serious Mistake May Have Been Made," CBS News, March 23, 2011, https://www.cbsnews.com/news/obama-on-gunwalking-serious-mistake-may-have-been-made/.

375 House Judiciary Committee Oversight with Eric Holder, C-SPAN, May 3, 2011, https://www.c-span.org/video/?299299-1/justice-department-oversight-part-1.

376 Seymour Hersh, "The Killing of Osama bin Laden," *London Review of Books* 37, no. 10, May 21, 2015, https://www.lrb.co.uk/the-paper/v37/n10/seymour-m.-hersh/the-killing-of-osama-bin-laden.

377 Carlotta Gall, "The Detail in Seymour Hersh's Bin Laden Story That Rings True," *New York Times*, May 12, 2015, https://www.nytimes.com/2015/05/12/magazine/the-detail-in-seymour-hershs-bin-laden-story-that-rings-true.html.

378 Robert M. Gates, *Duty: Memoirs of a Secretary at War* (New York: Alfred A. Knopf, 2014), 545.

379 *Worthy Fights*, 327.

380 *A Promised Land*, 699.

381 John Bresnahan and Seung Min Kim, "Holder Held in Contempt," *Politico*, June 28, 2012, https://www.politico.com/story/2012/06/holder-held-in-contempt-of-congress-077988.

382 Bob Bauer, "Michael Cohen Reminded Us Why Trump's Birtherism Matters," *Atlantic*, March 4, 2019, https://www.theatlantic.com/ideas/archive/2019/03/michael-cohens-testimony-shed-light-trumps-racism/584038/.

383 Alexander Burns and Jonathan Martin, "Joe Biden Announces 2020 Run for President, After Months of Hesitation," *New York Times*, April 25, 2019, https://www.nytimes.com/2019/04/25/us/politics/joe-biden-2020-announcement.html.

384 "'The President's Speech' at White House Correspondents' Dinner," The White House, May 1, 2011, https://obamawhitehouse.archives.gov/realitycheck/the-press-office/2011/05/01/remarks-president-white-house-correspondents-association-dinner.

385 Ann E. Marimow, "A Rare Peek into a Justice Department Leak Probe," *Washington Post*, May 19, 2013, https://www.washingtonpost.com/local/a-rare-peek-into-a-justice-department-leak-probe/2013/05/19/0bc473de-be5e-11e2-97d4-a479289a31f9_story.html?hpid=z2&tid=a_inl_manual.

386 Sharyl Attkisson, *Stonewalled: My Fight for Truth Against the Forces of Obstruction, Intimidation, and Harassment in Obama's Washington* (New York: HarperCollins, 2014), 298, Kindle edition.

387 Fred Johnson, "Insider Threat Program Hearkens to '1984,'" *Morgan Citizen,* June 28, 2013, https://morgancountycitizen.com/2013/06/28/insider-threat-program-hearkens-to-1984/.

388 James C. Goodale, "Only Nixon Harmed a Free Press More," *New York Times,* updated July 31, 2013, https://www.nytimes.com/roomfordebate/2013/05/21/obama-the-media-and-national-security/only-nixon-harmed-a-free-press-more.

389 *A Promised Land,* 458.

390 Ibid., 638.

391 Gary Younge, "'A Promised Land' by Barack Obama Review—an Impressive but Incomplete Memoir," *Guardian,* November 26, 2020, https://www.theguardian.com/books/2020/nov/26/a-promised-land-by-barack-obama-review-an-impressive-but-incomplete-memoir.

392 *A Promised Land,* 586.

393 Incident Report 9005127, Cambridge Police Department, July 16, 2009, http://s.wsj.net/public/resources/documents/GatesPoliceReport.pdf.

394 *A Promised Land,* 395.

395 Mike Royko, "Jesse Jackson's Message Is Too Advanced for Most," *Baltimore Sun,* December 3, 1993, https://www.baltimoresun.com/news/bs-xpm-1993-12-03-1993337169-story.html.

396 *A Promised Land,* 397.

397 Ibid., 398.

398 Daniel Patrick Moynihan, *The Negro Family: The Case for National Action*, US Department of Labor, March 1965, https://www.dol.gov/general/aboutdol/history/webid-moynihan/moynchapter5.

399 "Attorney General Eric Holder at the Department of Justice African American History Month Program," February 18, 2009, https://www.justice.gov/opa/speech/attorney-general-eric-holder-department-justice-african-american-history-month-program.

400 Heather Mac Donald, "Nation of Cowards?" *City-Journal,* February 19, 2009, https://www.city-journal.org/html/nation-cowards-10538.html.

401 "The Shared Agendas of George Soros & Barack Obama," Discover the Networks, last updated February 8, 2021, https://www.discoverthenetworks.org/organizations/the-shared-agendas-of-george-soros-barack-obama/.

402 Toby Harden, "Jesse Jackson Forced to Apologise Again to Barack Obama for Racist Slur," *Telegraph,* July 17, 2008, https://www.telegraph.co.uk/

news/worldnews/northamerica/usa/2420533/Jesse-Jackson-forced-to-apologise-again-for-racist-slur.html.

403 *Face the Nation*, CBS News, December 28, 2014, http://www.cbsnews.com/videos/rudy-giuliani-obama-signaling-hes-against-the-police/.

404 Michelle Ye Hee Lee, "Giuliani's Claim the White House Invited Al Sharpton Up to 85 Times," *Washington Post,* December 30, 2014, https://www.washingtonpost.com/news/fact-checker/wp/2014/12/30/giulianis-claim-the-white-house-invited-al-sharpton-up-to-85-times/.

405 Jake Tapper, "The Skeletons and Suits in Sharpton's Closet," *Salon*, June 21, 2003, https://www.salon.com/2003/06/21/sharpton_7/.

406 *A Promised Land*, 117.

407 Ibid., 37.

408 David Remnick, "Race and the Joshua Generation," *New Yorker,* November 17, 2008, https://www.newyorker.com/magazine/2008/11/17/the-joshua-generation.

409 *Becoming*, 197.

410 Ibid., 149.

411 Phil Boerner, "Barack Obama '83, My Columbia College Roommate," *Columbia College Today*, January/February 2009, https://www.college.columbia.edu/cct/archive/jan_feb09/alumni_corner.

412 *Becoming*, 172.

413 "Michelle Obama on Letterman: Shopping at Target Story," December 18, 2014, https://www.youtube.com/watch?v=L5H-LhiCpHw.

414 Sandra Sobieraj Westfall, "The Obamas: How We Deal with Our Own Racist Experiences," *People,* December 17, 2014, https://people.com/celebrity/the-obamas-how-we-deal-with-our-own-racist-experiences/.

415 *A Promised Land*, 133–134.

416 Katie Reilly, "Read Hillary Clinton's 'Basket of Deplorables' Remarks about Donald Trump Supporters," *Time,* September 10, 2016, https://time.com/4486502/hillary-clinton-basket-of-deplorables-transcript/.

417 *A Promised Land*, 407.

418 "Cornel West Takes on Obama," *Wall Street Journal*, May 20, 2011, https://www.wsj.com/articles/BL-SEB-65299.

419 Jodi Kantor and Jeff Zeleny, "Michelle Obama Adds New Role to Balancing Act," *New York Times*, May 18, 2007, https://www.nytimes.com/2007/05/18/us/politics/18michelle.html.

420 *Barack and Michelle*, 221.

421 *Becoming*, 160.

422 "Are We Getting Two for One?" *Slate.*

423 *Becoming,* 165.
424 "Obama, Clinton Speeches in Selma, Alabama," Transcripts, CNN.com, March 4, 2007, http://transcripts.cnn.com/TRANSCRIPTS/0703/04/le.02.html.
425 Neil King Jr. and Rebecca Ballhaus, "Views on Race Relations Sour, Especially among Blacks," *Wall Street Journal,* July 24, 2013, https:// www.wsj.com/articles/SB10001424127887324144304578624183 517587130.
426 "Views of Race Relations," Pew Research Center, July 27, 2016, https://www.pewsocialtrends.org/2016/06/27/2-views-of-race-relations/.
427 Timothy Burke, "Colin Kaepernick Refuses to Stand for Anthem: 'There Are Bodies in the Street,'" *Deadspin,* August 27, 2016, https://deadspin.com/colin-kapernick-refuses-to-stand-for-anthem-there-are-1785838030.
428 *Becoming,* 381.
429 Ibid., 396.
430 Don Babwin, "Chicago Ends 2020 with 769 Homicides as Gun Violence Surges," Associated Press, ABC New, January 1, 2021, https://abcnews.go.com/US/wireStory/chicago-ends-2020-769-homicides-gun-violence-surges-75005949.
431 Alexandra Svokos, "Former President Barack Obama Issues Statement on George Floyd," ABC News, May 29, 2020, https://abcnews.go.com/Politics/president-barack-obama-issues-statement-george-floyd/story?id=70954996.
432 Cheryl Corley, "Massive 1-Year Rise in Homicide Rates Collided with the Pandemic in 2020," NPR, January 6, 2021, https://www.npr.org/2021/01/06/953254623/massive-1-year-rise-in-homicide-rates-collided-with-the-pandemic-in-2020.

About the Author

An independent writer and producer, Jack Cashill has written a dozen nonfiction books and appeared on C-SPAN's *Book TV* ten times. He also produced a score of feature-length documentaries. Jack serves as executive editor of *Ingram's Magazine*. He writes regularly for *American Thinker*, *American Spectator*, and WorldNetDaily and has also written for the *Wall Street Journal*, *Fortune*, the *Washington Post*, and the *Weekly Standard*. Jack has a Ph.D. from Purdue University in American studies and has taught at a French university under the auspices of the Fulbright program.